Prelude to The Lesser Peace

Kathy Lee

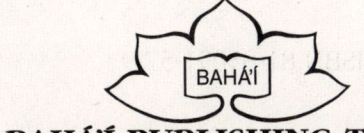

Bahá'í Publishing Trust
P. O. Box No. 19
New Delhi 110 001, India

© The National Spiritual Assembly
of the Bahá'ís of India

First Edition 1989

ISBN 81-85091-57-9

Printed at Mehta Offset, New Delhi-110 028
Filmset at Navyug Phototype Setters Pvt. Ltd.
Pune-411 030

DEDICATION

To my parents, Ralph and Shirley Lee, for instilling in me the desire to work for peace, and to my children, Jamál and Rúḥí, and their generation, for whose peace and well-being we have labored, and who are destined to carry forward the torch of peace, I bequeath this book.

ACKNOWLEDGEMENTS

Prelude to the Lesser Peace did not begin as a book. The idea of exploring what must occur before the Lesser Peace is established was first conceived while listening to talks given by Mr. Alí Nakhjavání at Green Acre Bahá'í School in 1980. The subject required much research. In the process of doing the research, I presented the accumulating material to several summer and winter schools over a period of about six years.

In 1982 our family pioneered to Bophuthatswana. After presenting several courses on the subject in Southern Africa, the Bahá'ís encouraged me to organize the references in book form in order to make it easier for the friends to study the subject in one book rather than having to search through several books in order to find the full range of references available. Seeing that many of the friends did not have access to a complete Bahá'í library, I endeavored to organize the material in a very straightforward presentation. Therefore, this work is primarily a compilation of Bahá'í references with additional thoughts and comments from Mr. Nakhjavání and myself. It is not, however, an exhaustive presentation of the writings on the subject, as there are many other references not included here.

I want to express my appreciation to Mr. Nakhjavání for having encouraged the writing of this book and for allowing his material to be included in the book.

ACKNOWLEDGEMENTS

My special appreciation also goes to Steve and Judy Worth and Suhayl Rawhání for their assuming responsibility for the financing of the first typing of the manuscript and for their continual encouragement throughout the writing of the book. For the second typing, I sincerely thank Susie Simerly. For technical assistance with word processing, I thank Jack Henderson. For sustained encouragement and support during the entire period of research, writing, and editing I thank Mary K. Rádpour. In addition, I wish to thank my children Rúḥí and Jamál, for reminding me by virtue of their very existence, of my obligation as a mother to endeavor ceaselessly for the inauguration of global peace for the sake of present and future generations.

Kathy Lee
June 22, 1988

CONTENTS

List of Tables vii
Abbreviations ix
Introduction 1

CHAPTER ONE

The Vision: A Peaceful Earth 5

    The Inevitability of World Peace 5

    Biblical Prophecies of World Peace 5

    The Establisher of the Most Great Peace . . . 7

    Evolution Toward Universal Peace 10

    The Most Great Peace —
    The Ultimate Goal 12

    Essentials of a Divine Economy 18

    Humanity's Coming of Age 19

    The Nature of Man and
    the Most Great Peace 22

    The Kingdom of God on Earth 24

    The Lesser Peace 25

    Ages — Past, Present and Future 27

CHAPTER TWO

The Formative Age: The Age of Transition . . 29

- The Integrating Process 29
  - *Some Objectives of the Formative Age* 31
  - *The Major and Minor Plans of God* 33
- The Disintegrating Process 35
  - *From Adolescence to Maturity* 36
  - *An Age of Travail* 37
- The Fruits of Suffering 39
  - *The Need for Spiritual Midwives* 45

CHAPTER THREE

Outstanding Events of The Formative Age . . 47

- Let Them be Swept Away 47
  - *The Collapse of Empires* 47
  - *The Decline of Islám* 48
  - *The Deterioration of Christian Institutions* . . 51
  - *Signs of Moral Downfall* 53
  - *The Breakdown of Political and Economic Structure* 55
- Wars — Causes and Consequences 57
  - *World War I* 57
  - *The League of Nations* 60
  - *World War II* 63

CONTENTS

    The United Nations 65
    Post World War II 66

CHAPTER FOUR
The Lesser Peace 75

    Established by the Nations of the Earth . . 75
    Principles and Features of the Lesser Peace . . 76
    Steps Leading to the Lesser Peace 77
    The First and the Fifth Candles of Unity 81
    During the Twentieth Century 91

    Contributing Factors to the Lesser Peace . . 93
    The Supreme Tribunal 93
    America Prepared for Preponderating Role . . 96
    The Retributive Calamity 102
    The Nature of the Calamity 103

CHAPTER FIVE
Calamities: Prelude to The Lesser Peace . . .105

    Disunity a Danger 105
    The Necessity of Upheavals 105
    Retribution 106
    Sins of Omission and Commission 106
    Chastisement for Human Perversity 108
    The Lamentably Defective Present Order . . .109

    Out of His Love 110

    Rites of Passage 111

    A Fitting Climax 112

CHAPTER SIX

Developing Constructive Responses to Calamities 113

    Probable Reactions 113

    Sustaining Concepts 114

    The Transforming Power of the Cause of God .114

    The End in the Beginning 117

    Steps for Handling the Stress of
    Worldwide Afflictions 120

    Prayer: From Doubt into Certainty 120

    'Abdu'l-Bahá, The Exemplar 122

    Serve the Cause and Teach 123

    Single-minded Devotion 126

CHAPTER SEVEN

Opposition to The Faith of Bahá'u'lláh . . .129

    Why Must There be Opposition? 129

    Who Will Attack the Faith? 132

    How Will the Cause be Opposed? 133

    Who Will Defend or Protect the Faith? 134

    Hidden Springs of Celestial Strength 136

CONTENTS

CHAPTER EIGHT

Cultivating Spiritual Responses to Opposition 137

    The Fruits of Opposition — Re-framing our Perspective 137

    The Rhythm of Growth 139

    "After the Storm..." 141

    Behavior Toward the Oppressors 142

    'Abdu'l-Bahá in Times of Persecution 143

    Bahá'ís in Irán — Living Testimonials 149

    Spiritual Endurance Releases Forces 156

    May We Be Worthy 158

CHAPTER NINE

Women: The Missing Factor in Establishing Peace 159

    Creating the Climate for Peace 159

    Mothers and Peace 161

    Education: First Priority to Women 164

    The Responsibility of Men to Encourage Women 165

    The Responsibility of Women to Develop Themselves 166

    The Right to Vote 167

    Women's Superior Capacities 169

    Women Arising for Peace 170

CHAPTER TEN

Our Children and Youth in the Age of Frustration 171

   The Promise and the Threat 173

     The Promise 174

     The Threat 174

   Growing Up 178

   Words as Mild as Milk 178

     Keeping the Perspective 180

     Inheritors of the Lesser Peace 180

     Youth 181

Epilogue 187

Bibliography 189

LIST OF TABLES

Table One
    Bahá'í Commonwealth 17

Table Two
    Development of the Faith 21

Table Three
    Ages of the Bahá'í Era 27

Table Four
    Formative Age 32

Table Five
    Plans of God: Major and Minor 34

Table Six
    The Lesser Peace 89

ABBREVIATIONS

ABL	'Abdu'l-Bahá in London
ADJ	The Advent of Divine Justice
AHW	Arabic Hidden Words. See The Hidden Words of Bahá'u'lláh.
BA	Bahá'í Administration
BP	Bahá'í Prayers
BW	The Bahá'í World, Volume XV
BWF	Bahá'í World Faith
CF	Citadel of Faith
CFH	A Cry from the Heart
DAL	The Divine Art of Living
DFE	The Dynamic Force of Example
GPB	God Passes By
HW	The Hidden Words of Bahá'u'lláh
KI	Kitáb-i-Iqán
LG	Lights of Guidance
MA	Messages to America
MBW	Messages to the Bahá'í World

MUHJ	Messages from the Universal House of Justice
OMF	The Onward March of the Faith
PDC	The Promised Day is Come
PP	The Priceless Pearl
PT	Paris Talks
PUP	The Promulgation of Universal Peace
PWP	The Promise of World Peace
SAQ	Some Answered Questions
SDC	The Secret of Divine Civilization
SV	The Seven Valleys and the Four Valleys
SW	Star of the West
SWA	Selections from the Writings of 'Abdu'l-Bahá
TA	Tablets of 'Abdu'l-Bahá
TB	Tablets of Bahá'u'lláh
VP	Victory Promises
WG	Wellspring of Guidance
WO	World Order
WOB	The World Order of Bahá'u'lláh

INTRODUCTION

This book focuses on those processes which are at work in the Age of Transition and which are propelling humanity towards the Lesser Peace. It explores the meaning of the tumult of our times in light of mankind's ordained destiny, the nature of the choices placed before this generation, the consequences of those choices, and the remaining challenges facing us before reaching the Lesser Peace. Its purpose is to assist the Bahá'ís to understand both the causes and the benefits of the turmoil and suffering of this Age of Frustration so that we may participate in our society-building efforts and avoid the despair and hopelessness suffered by those who are unaware of the fruits which will be borne at the end of this period of world-embracing tribulations.

With regard to the Writings of the Guardian of the Bahá'í Faith, Shoghi Effendi labored for thirty-six years, between 1921 and 1957, to provide the Bahá'ís of the world with all the essential guidance necessary to live in this Age of Transition with a true and deep understanding of its nature, processes, trends, ordeals, and blessings. I regard his writings and letters containing such illumination as a work of compassion. For him to have taken such pains under circumstances often adverse to his own health and well-being and while simultaneously managing the multitudinous affairs of a world religion, demonstrates to me the deep commitment he had to our education regarding the nature of the age in which we live. It also reveals his deep sense of compassion for humanity passing through the "dark heart" of the Age of Transition. Therefore, I have attempted to gather together some of Shoghi Effendi's writings on the nature of the Age of Transition, the course it will follow, the world-wide upheavals which must occur prior to the inception of the Lesser Peace, and those Writings from the three Central Figures and The Universal House of Justice which provide guidance regarding how to cope with the tests and difficulties of this period.

In addition to the sacred texts and works of the beloved Guardian and The Universal House of Justice, I have included some of the pertinent thoughts of Mr. Alí Nakhjavání who has studied this particular aspect of the Bahá'í literature in depth.

Throughout this book one will find a recurring use of the analogy of the midwife who assists the expectant mother at the time of her impending labor and childbirth. This analogy was chosen because of the many references in the Bahá'í Writings to this age being a "travailing age." "The whole earth is now in a state of pregnancy. The day is approaching when it will have yielded its noblest fruits..." (WOB 169) As society is currently carrying within its womb the well-nigh full-term fetus, and will soon enter a period of intense labor, followed by the birth of the Lesser Peace, the role of the midwife comes into light. The midwife must assist the laboring mother to understand what is happening, particularly if the mother is uninformed about the processes of labor and childbirth. The midwife comforts and calms the fears and anxieties in the mother as her pain and labor deepen and intensify. The midwife encourages the mother to co-operate with those unrelenting natural forces inexorably propelling forward the new life carried within her.

It seems to me that the Bahá'ís of the world are like the spiritual midwives to a toiling humanity, unaware of the fruit to which it will soon give birth. As the global upheavals and afflictions become more severe, as the earth approaches her time of delivering the Lesser Peace, the Bahá'ís must stand ready to lend assistance to every heavy heart, to every discouraged soul, to every afflicted member of humanity's "Age of Frustration." (WOB 171) We must explain to the disillusioned the purpose for the world's afflictions. We must point out the pathway to the Lesser Peace with vision and certitude, fully conscious that the path is strewn with thorns, precipices, obstacles, and setbacks, yet absolutely confident that the obstacles are surmountable and that the major plan of God is unfolding. We must transmit our knowledge that the earth will cast forth her burden by the end of the twentieth century with the inception of the Lesser Peace, through the fires of suffering and experience. We must evince in our own attitude that whatever suffering humanity must undergo is for our own perfecting and will produce a momentous and significant step forward in the historic evolution of mankind, and that the product, which will be the initial stage of peace on earth, is worth any ordeal through which mankind will have to pass.

After the ordeal of labor and childbirth, every mother greets her new child with a radiant heart, grateful for having seen the process through to the end. And to the midwife, the mother owes her heartfelt and boundless gratitude for the invaluable help she received when she was at her hour of greatest distress.

CHAPTER ONE

The Vision : A Peaceful Earth

THE INEVITABILITY OF WORLD PEACE

"To the Peoples of the World:
The Great Peace towards which people of good will throughout the centuries have inclined their hearts, of which seers and poets for countless generations have expressed their vision, and for which from age to age the sacred scriptures of mankind have constantly held the promise, is now at long last within the reach of the nations. For the first time in history it is possible for everyone to view the entire planet, with all its myriad diversified peoples, in one perspective. World peace is not only possible but inevitable. It is the next stage in the evolution of this planet — in the words of one great thinker, 'the planetization of mankind'."

(PWP 1)

Biblical Prophecies of World Peace

Universal peace has been the vision promised in all of the religions of the past. It has been described as "the destiny which mankind must, at its stage of maturity achieve." To cite one prophet of the Old Testament, Isaiah prophesied —

"And He (the Lord) shall judge among the nations and shall rebuke many people: and they shall beat their swords into plowshares and their spears into pruning hooks: nation shall not lift up sword against nation, neither shall they learn war any more."

(Isaiah 2:4)

This general dscription of the coming of a time when weapons of destruction will be transformed into implements of progress and tranquility for humanity is followed by another glimpse of a peaceful planet in Isaiah 11:6-9 —

"The wolf also shall dwell with the lamb, and the leopard shall lie down with the kid; and the calf and the young lion and the fatling together; and a little child shall lead them. And the cow and the bear shall feed; their young ones shall lie down together; and the lion shall eat straw like the ox. And the sucking child shall play on the hole of the asp, and the weaned child shall put his hand on the cockatrice's den. They shall not hurt nor destroy in all my holy mountain; for the earth shall be full of the knowledge of the Lord, as the waters cover the sea."

As 'Abdu'l-Bahá explains —

"...the leopard and the lamb, the lion and the calf, the child and the asp, are metaphors and symbols for various nations, peoples, antagonistic sects and hostile races, who are as opposite and inimical as the wolf and the lamb."

(SAQ 63)

"The relations between the countries — the mingling, union and friendship of the peoples and communities — will reach to such a degree that the human race will be like one family and kindred. The light of heavenly love will shine, and the darkness of enmity and hatred will be dispelled from the world.

Universal peace will raise its tent in the center of the earth, and the blessed Tree of Life will grow and spread to such an extent that it will overshadow the East and the West. Strong and weak, rich and poor, antagonistic sects and hostile nations which are like the wolf and the lamb, the leopard and the kid, the lion and the calf — will act toward each other with the most complete love, friendship, justice and equity."

(SAQ 64)

About Isaiah's prophecy, 'Abdu'l-Bahá also says —

"It means that fierce and contending religions, hostile creeds, and divergent beliefs will reconcile and associate, notwithstanding their former hatreds and antagonisms. Through the liberalism of human attitude demanded in this radiant century they will blend together in perfect fellowship and love. This is the spirit and meaning of Isaiah's words. There will never be a day when this prophecy will come to pass literally, for these animals by their natures cannot mingle and associate in kindness and love. Therefore, this prophecy symbolizes the unity and agreement of races, nations and peoples who will come together in attitudes of intelligence, illumination and spirituality."

(PUP 369-70)

The Establisher of the Most Great Peace

The Bringer of such a peaceful period is also alluded to by the same Old Testament prophet:

"For unto us a child is born, unto us a son is given: and the government shall be upon his shoulder: and his name shall be called Wonderful, Counsellor, the

Mighty God, the Everlasting Father, the Prince of Peace. Of the increase of his government and peace there shall be no end, upon the throne of David, and upon his kingdom, to order it, and to establish it with judgement and with justice from henceforth for ever and ever. The zeal of the Lord of hosts will perform this.

(Isaiah 9:6-7)

And more specifically in Isaiah 11:1-5 —

"And there shall come forth a rod out of the stem of Jesse and a branch shall grow out of his roots: and the spirit of the Lord shall rest upon him, the spirit of wisdom and understanding, the spirit of counsel and might, the spirit of knowledge and of the fear of the Lord; ...And he shall smite the earth with the rod of his mouth, and with the breath of his lips shall he slay the wicked. And righteousness shall be the girdle of his loins, and faithfulness the girdle of his reins."

According to Shoghi Effendi, both of these prophecies of Isaiah refer to Bahá'u'lláh.

"He derived his descent, on the one hand, from Abraham (the Father of the Faithful) through his wife Katurah, and on the other from zoroaster, as well as from Yazdigird, the last king of the Sásáníyán dynasty. He was moreover a descendant of Jesse, and belonged, through His father, Mírzá Abbás, better known as Mírzá Buzurg...to one of the most ancient and renowned of families of Mázindarán."

(GPB 94)

"To Him [Bahá'u'lláh] Isaiah, the greatest of the Jewish prophets, had alluded as the 'Glory of the Lord,' the 'Everlasting Father,' the 'Prince of Peace,' the

'Wonderful,' the 'Counsellor,' the 'Rod come forth out of the stem of Jesse' and the 'Branch grown out of His roots,' Who shall be established upon the throne of David, Who 'will come with strong hand,' Who 'shall judge among the nations,' Who 'shall smite the earth with the rod of His mouth, and with the breath of His lips slay the wicked,' and Who 'shall assemble the outcasts of Israel, and gather together the dispersed of Judah from the four corners of the earth.'"

(GPB 94-95)

To Christendom He was —
"Christ returned 'in the glory of the Father,' to S͟hí'ah Islám, the return of Imám Husayn; to the Zoroastrians, the promised S͟háh-Bahrám; to the Hindus, the reincarnation of Krishna; to the Buddhists, the fifth Buddha."

(GPB 94)

More specific titles of Bahá'u'lláh are penned by the beloved Guardian. He is the —
"One Whom posterity will acclaim as...the Judge, the Lawgiver and Redeemer of all mankind, as the Organizer of the entire planet, as the Unifier of the children of men, as the Inaugurator of the long-awaited millennium, as the Originator of the new 'Universal Cycle,' as the Establisher of the Most Great Peace, as the Fountain of the Most Great Justice, as the Proclaimer of the coming of age of the entire human race, as the Creator of a new World Order, and as the Inspirer and Founder of a world civilization."

(GPB 93-94)

Evolution Toward Universal Peace

It is a Bahá'í teaching that:

> "...All the divine Manifestations have proclaimed the oneness of God and the unity of mankind. They have taught that men should love and mutually help each other in order that they might progress...The fundamental truth of the Manifestations is peace. This underlies all religion, all justice. The divine purpose is that men should live in unity, concord and agreement and should love one another."
>
> (PUP 32)

It is because of this basic principle that all religions have come to lead mankind ultimately to peace, that there are so many prophecies regarding peace in all the Holy Books. But the road to peace, as voiced by the Prophets of all religions, is gradual and painstaking. The process of social, economic, political integration —

> "...which, starting with the family, the smallest unit in the scale of human organization, must, after having called successively into being the tribe, the city-state, and the nation, continue to operate until it culminates in the unification of the whole world, the final object and the crowning glory of human evolution on this planet. It is this stage which humanity, ...is resistlessly approaching... It is with this stage that the fortunes and the purpose of the Faith of Bahá'u'lláh are indissolubly linked."
>
> (PDC 118)

Although the purpose of all past religions was to pave the way and lay the foundations for universal peace and the unification of the whole world, it is the central theme of the teachings of Bahá'u'lláh —

> "In every Dispensation the light of Divine Guidance has been focused upon one central theme... In this

wondrous Revelation, this glorious century, the foundation of the Faith of God, and the distinguishing feature of His Law, is the consciousness of the oneness of mankind."

(PDC 119)

"The Revelation associated with Faith of Jesus Christ focused attention primarily on the redemption of the individual and the molding of his conduct, and stressed as its central theme, the necessity of inculcating a high standard of morality and discipline into man, as the fundamental unit in human society. Nowhere in the Gospels do we find any reference to the unity of nations or the unification of mankind as a whole."

(PDC 119)

"The Faith of Islám, the succeeding link in chain of Divine Revelation, introduced, as Bahá'u'lláh Himself testifies, the conception of the nations as a unit and a vital stage in the organization of human society, and embodied it in its teaching. This indeed is what is meant by this brief yet highly significant and illuminating pronouncement of Bahá'u'lláh: 'Of old (Islamic Dispensation) it hath been revealed: "Love of one's country is an element of the Faith of God."' This principle was established and stressed by the Apostle of God, inasmuch as the evolution of human society required it at that time. Nor could any stage above and beyond it have been envisioned, as world conditions preliminary to the establishment of a superior form of organization were as yet unobtainable. The conception of nationality, the attainment to the state of nationhood, may, therefore, be said to be the distinguishing characteristics of the Muhammadan Dispensation..."

(PDC 120)

"One of the great events which is to occur in the day of the manifestation of that Incomparable Branch (Bahá'u'lláh) is the hoisting of the Standard of God among all nations. By this is meant that all nations and kindreds will be gathered together under the shadow of this Divine Banner, which is no other than the Lordly Branch itself, and will become a single nation. Religious and sectarian antagonism, the hostility of races and peoples, and differences among nations, will be eliminated. All men will adhere to one religion, will have one common faith, will be blended into one race, and become a single people. All will dwell in one common fatherland, which is the planet itself."

(SAQ 65)

"This is the stage which the world is now approaching, the stage of world unity, which as 'Abdu'l-Bahá assures us, will, in this century, be securely established. 'The Tongue of Grandeur', Bahá'u'lláh Himself affirms, 'hath...in the Day of His Manifestation proclaimed: It is not his to boast who loveth his country, but it is his who loveth the world.' "

(PDC 121)

THE MOST GREAT PEACE – THE ULTIMATE GOAL

Alluding to the Most Great Peace in His Tablet to Queen Victoria, Bahá'u'lláh has declared: —

"That which the Lord hath ordained as the sovereign remedy and mightiest instrument for the healing of

The Vision : A Peaceful Earth

all the world is the union of all its peoples in one universal Cause, one common Faith. This can in nowise be achieved except through the power of a skilled, an all-powerful and inspired Physician."

(WOB 163)

The Guardian points out that it is the mission of the Revelation of Bahá'u'lláh to achieve the organic and spiritual unity of the whole body of nations and this will signalize the coming of age of the entire human race. The Most Great Peace will be one that —

"...must inevitably follow as the practical consequence of the spiritualization of the world and the fusion of all its races, creeds, classes and nations — can rest on no other basis, and can be preserved through no other agency, except the divinely appointed ordinances that are implicit in the World Order that stands associated with His Holy Name."

(WOB 162-163)

In one of his talks dated December 25, 1984, Mr. Alí Nakhjavání stated —

"...Shoghi Effendi is reported to have told pilgrims that the Golden Age and the Most Great Peace would occur towards the end of the Dispensation of Bahá'u'lláh. In any case, in his foreward to ***God Passes By***, he clearly states that it would be in the course of 'succeeding centuries' that the world-embracing Bahá'í Commonwealth of the future will emerge."

Mr. Nakhjavání said that in 1936 in his "Unfoldment of World Civilization" and in subsequent letters, the Guardian taught us that the Most Great Peace involved the following —

"1. the recognition of the character, and acknowledgement of the claims, of the Faith of Bahá'u'lláh;
2. the spiritualization of the masses;
3. the fusion of all races, creeds, classes, and nations;
4. the direct operation of the laws and principles of Bahá'u'lláh;
5. the functioning of The Universal House of Justice as the supreme organ of the Bahá'í super-state;
6. the birth of a world civilization to be perpetuated in future Dispensations — an earthly heaven, capable of mirroring forth the splendors of the Abhá Kingdom — the hallmark of the inception of the Golden Age of Bahá'u'lláh."

(Nakhjavání, 1984)

The Guardian provides further elucidation on the principles which will form the broad foundation of a lasting global peace in The *World Order of Bahá'u'lláh* –

"The unity of the human race, as envisaged by Bahá'u'lláh implies the establishment of a world commonwealth in which all nations, races, creeds and classes are closely and permanently united, and in which the autonomy of its state members and personal freedom and initiative of the individuals that compose them are definitely and completely safeguarded. This commonwealth must, as far as we can visualize it, consist of a world legislature, whose members will, as the trustees of the whole of mankind, ultimately control the entire resources of all the component nations, and will enact such laws as shall be required to regulate the life, satisfy the needs and adjust the relationships of all races and peoples. A world executive, backed by an international Force, will carry out the decisions arrived at, and apply the laws enacted by, this world legislature, and will safeguard the organic unity of the whole commonwealth. A world tribunal will adjudicate and deliver its compulsory and final verdict in all and any disputes that may arise between the various elements constituting this universal system. A mechanism of world inter-communication will be devised, embracing the whole planet, free from national hindrances and restrictions, and functioning with marvelous swiftness and perfect regularity. A world metropolis will act as the nerve center of a world civilization, the focus towards which the unifying forces of life will converge and from its energizing influences will radiate. A world language will either be invented or chosen from amoung the existing languages and will be taught in the schools of all the federated nations as an auxiliary to their mother tongue. A world script, a world literature, a uniform and universal system of currency, of weights and measures, will simplify and facilitate intercourse and understanding among the nations and races of mankind. In such a world society, science and religion, the two most potent forces in human life, will be reconciled, will cooperate, and will harmoniously develop. The press will, under such a system, while giving full scope of the expression of the diversified views and convictions of mankind, cease to be mischievously manipulated by vested interests, whether private or public, and will be liberated from the influence of contending governments and peoples. The economic resources of the world will be organized, its sources of raw materials will be tapped and fully utilized, its markets will be coordinated and developed, and the distribution of its products will be equitably regulated.

"National rivalries, hatreds, and intrigues will cease, and racial animosity and prejudice be replaced by racial amity, understanding and cooperation. The causes of religious strife will be permanently removed, economic barriers and restrictions will be completely abolished and the inordinate distinction between classes will be obliterated. Destitution on the one hand, and gross accumulation of ownership on the other will disappear. The enormous energy dissipated and wasted on war, whether economic or political, will be consecrated to such ends as will extend the range of human inventions and technical development, to the increase of the productivity of mankind, the extermination of disease, to the extension of scientific research, to the raising of the standard of physical health, to the sharpening and refinement of the human brain, to the exploitation of the unused and unsuspected resources of the planet, to the prolongation of human life, and to the furtherance of any other agency that can stimulate the intellectual, the moral, and spiritual life of the entire human race.

"A world federal system, ruling the whole earth and exercising unchallengeable authority over its unimaginably vast resources, blending and embodying the ideals of both the East and the West, liberated from the curse of war and its miseries, and bent on the exploitation of all the available sources of energy on the surface of the planet, a system in which Force is made the servant of Justice, whose life is sustained by its universal recognition of one God and by its allegiance to one common Revelation — such is the goal towards which humanity, impelled by the unifying forces of life, is moving."

(WOB 203-204) (See Table 1)

TABLE ONE

Bahá'í Commonwealth

1. World executive branch
2. World parliament
3. World tribunal
4. Individual freedom protected
5. World intercommunication
6. World language
7. World metropolis
8. World script/literature
9. Common currency, weights, measures
10. Science and religion in harmony
11. World press
12. Economics reorganized
13. Markets coordinated
14. Distribution regulated
15. Inventions, technology extended
16. Disease exterminated
17. Scientific research
18. Health standards raised
19. Human brain refined
20. Sustained and inspired by Revelation of Bahá'u'lláh

(WOB 203-4)

"So, such is the picture we get about the Most Great Peace. The Lesser Peace falls short of these conditions, and among these the primary condition is the recognition of Bahá'u'lláh as the Manifestation of

God for today. This is a very important point for us to remember as we proceed in our study of this subject."

(Na<u>kh</u>javání, 1984)

It is also clear from the above passages that the most Great Peace will appear in the Golden Age of the Bahá'í Dispensation, after centuries of evolution.

Essentials of a Divine Economy

The vision of the Prophets of God regarding the establishment of universal peace has been painted in broad strokes in the Holy Books of the past, but as we study the above passages, we see that Bahá'u'lláh has provided us with graphic details about the structure and the spirit of that Golden Age and the Most Great Peace. He assumes responsibility for providing humanity with all the essential teachings to establish world peace —

"The Most Great Peace...as conceived by Bahá'u'lláh — a peace that must inevitably follow as the practical consequence of the spiritualization of the world and the fusion of all its races, creeds, classes, and nations — can rest on no other basis, and can, be preserved through no other agency, except the divinely appointed ordinances that are implicit in the World Order that stands associated with His Holy Name."

(WOB 162-163)

Not only does Bahá'u'lláh supply the essential concepts and principles required for world peace, he also has created new institutions whose mission is to usher in peace —

"For Bahá'u'lláh, we should readily recognize, has not only imbued mankind with a new and regenerating

Spirit. He has not merely enunciated certain universal principles, or propounded a particular philosophy, however potent, sound and universal these may be. In addition to these He, as well as 'Abdu'l-Bahá after Him, has, unlike the Dispensations of the past, clearly and specifically laid down a set of Laws, established definite institutions, and provided for the essentials of a Divine Economy. These are destined to be a pattern for future society, a supreme instrument for the establishment of the Most Great Peace, and the one agency for the unification of the world, and the proclamation of the reign of righteousness and justice upon the earth. Not only have they revealed all the directions required for the practical realization of those ideals which the Prophets of God have visualized, and which from time immemorial have inflamed the imagination of seers and poets in every age. They have also, in unequivocal and emphatic language appointed those twin institutions of the House of Justice and of the Guardianship as Their Chosen successors, destined to apply the principles, promulgate the laws, protect the institutions, adapt loyally and intelligently the Faith to the requirements of progressive society, and consummate the incorruptible inheritance which the Founders of the Faith have bequeathed to the world."

(WOB 19-20)

Humanity's Coming of Age

That it is the primary purpose of Bahá'u'lláh's Revelation to lead humanity to peace is attested to in the following passage: —

"The revelation of Bahá'u'lláh, whose supreme mission is none other but the achievement of this organic and spiritual unity of the whole body of nations, should, if we be faithful to its implications be regarded as signalizing through its advent the *coming of age of the entire human race*. It should be viewed not merely as yet another spiritual revival in the ever changing fortunes of mankind, not only as a further stage in a chain of progressive Revelations, nor even as the culmination of one of a series of recurrent prophetic cycles, but rather as marking the last and highest stage in the stupendous evolution of man's collective life on this planet. The emergence of a world community, the consciousness of world citizenship, the founding of a world civilization and culture — all of which must synchronize with the initial stages in the unfoldment of the Golden Age of the Bahá'í Era — should, by their very nature, be regarded as far as this planetary life is concerned, as the furthermost limits in the organization of human society, though man, as an individual, will, nay must indeed as a result of such a consummation, continue indefinitely to progress and develop."

(WOB 163)

There are several stages which the nascent institutions of the Bahá'í Faith must pass through before that most glorious level of peace, the Most Great Peace, can come into being —

"...the multitudinous issues that must be faced, the obstacles that must be overcome, and the responsibilities that must be assumed, to enable a sore-tried Faith to pass through the successive stage of unmitigated obscurity, of active repression, and of complete emancipation, leading in turn to its being acknowledged as an independent Faith, enjoying the status of full equality with its sister religions, to be followed by its establishment and recognition as a state religion, which in turn must give way to its assumption of the rights and prerogatives associated with the Bahá'í state, functioning in the plenitude of its powers, a stage which must ultimately culminate in the emergence of a world-wide Bahá'í Commonwealth, animated wholly by the spirit, and operating solely in direct conformity with the laws and principles of Bahá'u'lláh."

(ADJ 15) (See Table 2)

TABLE TWO

Development of The Faith

1. Unmitigated obscurity
2. Active repression
3. Complete emancipation
4. Independent equal status
5. State religion
6. Bahá'í State
7. World-wide Bahá'í Commonwealth

(ADJ 15)

And finally, an indication that the Most Great Peace will be under the leadership of The Universal House of Justice, the beloved Guardian explains: —

"Not only will present day Spiritual Assemblies be styled differently in the future, but they will be enabled also to add to their present functions those powers, duties, and prerogatives necessitated by the recognition of the Faith of Bahá'u'lláh, not merely as one of the recognized religious systems of the world, but as the State Religion of an independent and Sovereign Power. And as the Bahá'í Faith permeates the masses of the peoples of East and West, and its truth is embraced by the majority of the peoples of a number of the sovereign states of the world, will the Universal House of Justice attain the plenitude of its power and exercise, as the supreme organ of the Bahá'í Commonwealth, all the rights, the duties, and responsibilities incumbent upon the world's future super-state."

(WOB 7)

The Nature of Man and the Most Great Peace

Within the Writings of Bahá'u'lláh we are reminded of our true spiritual nature —
"O Son of Man!
Veiled in My immemorial being and in the ancient eternity of My essence, I knew love for thee; therefore I created thee, have engraved on thee Mine image and revealed to thee My beauty."

(AHW no. 3)

"Having created the world and all that liveth and moveth therein, He, through the direct operation of His unconditioned and sovereign Will, chose to confer upon man the unique distinction and capacity to know Him and to love Him — a capacity that must needs be regarded as the generating impulse and the primary purpose underlying the whole of creation... Upon the inmost reality of each and every created thing He hath shed the light of one of His names, and made it a recipient of the glory of one of His attributes. Upon the reality of man, however, He hath focused the radiance of all of His names and attributes, and made it a mirror of His own Self. Alone of all created things man hath been singled out for so great a favor, so enduring a bounty."

(GL 65)

"The Great Being saith: Regard man as a mine rich in gems of inestimable value. Education can, alone, cause it to reveal its treasures, and enable mankind to benefit therefrom."

(GL 260)

Having created us in His Own image, blessed us with a capacity to know and love Him, and enabled man to acquire and reflect all of His names and attributes, He has sent His Manifestations to guide and train us in order that we might fulfil our capacities and develop our spiritual qualities. The nature of the teachings of all the Prophets has been twofold: the one area of teachings is spiritual and designed to uplift the soul of man. The other set of teachings is social and is designed to create an environment in which the soul of man can flourish.

"God's purpose in sending His Prophets unto men is twofold. The first is to liberate the children of men from the darkness of ignorance, and guide them to the light of true understanding. The second is to ensure the peace and tranquility of mankind, and provide all the means by which they can be established."

(GL 79-80)

Today, because humanity is spiritually and mentally approaching its "age of maturity," a social environment which is also mature, must be evolved. That is why a global, peaceful order is required so that the fullness of the human spirit may be developed and enabled to express itself in its highest form thus far. Bahá'u'lláh has brought all the means required to establish such an environment.

The nature of the future Most Great Peace as envisioned by Bahá'u'lláh will be freed from all forms of prejudice which can prevent whole groups of people from expressing their intellectual, spiritual, creative talents. Humanity will be released from the exorbitant drainage of natural and human resources which the exploits of war demand. It will have economic, social, spiritual and administrative institutions which will operate in harmony with principles of world unity and the spiritual nature of man. An atmosphere conducive to the growth and development of all aspects of the human nature will be created — a global home fit for the soul of man. The society will correspond in spirit and form to the noble nature of man.

The Kingdom of God on Earth

The references cited in the beginning of this chapter from Isaiah refer to the coming of a peaceful, spiritual society. From the New Testament the concept is repeated in the Lord's Prayer, "...Thy Kingdom come, Thy will be done on earth as it is in heaven." The writer of the Apocalypse has similarly testified: "And I saw a new heaven and a new earth..."

As we review some of the Bahá'í Writings we find a number of terms referring to that time of world unity, when human society will have reached its highest level of global organization which will reflect God's purpose for man. Some of the names for this period which are indicated in the Bahá'í Writings are: the Golden Age, the World Civilization the Commonwealth of Nations, the World Order of Bahá'u'lláh, the Bahá'í Commonwealth, the Divine Polity, Federation of Mankind, and the Most Great Peace. These are synonymous with the biblical terms referring to the coming of the Kingdom of God and indicate the coming together of all nations, races, creeds, and religions.

THE LESSER PEACE

Prior to the Most Great Peace, the world will establish the Lesser Peace.

"No machinery falling short of the standard inculcated by the Bahá'í Revelation, and at variance with the sublime pattern ordained in His teachings, which the collective efforts of mankind may yet devise can ever hope to achieve anything above or beyond that 'Lesser Peace' to which the Author of our Faith has Himself alluded in His Writings. 'Now that ye have refused the Most Great Peace,' He admonishing the kings and rulers of the earth, has written, 'hold ye fast unto this the Lesser Peace, that haply ye may in some degree better your own condition and that of your dependents.' Expatiating on this Lesser Peace, He thus addresses in that same Tablet the rulers of the earth: 'Be reconciled among yourselves, that ye may need no more armaments save in a measure to safeguard your territories and dominions... Be united, O Kings of the earth, for thereby will the tempest of discord be stilled amongst you, and your peoples find rest, if ye be of them that comprehend. Should anyone among you take up arms against another, rise ye all against him, for this is naught but manifest justice.' "

(WOB 162)

Mr. Nakhjavání in his aforementioned talk, explained that this refers to the machinery devised by the political efforts of mankind to establish a peace among the nations by reducing national armaments and upholding the principles of collective security. It is the first phase of global peace which will unfold in successive stages to reach its final efflorescence in the Most Great Peace, and it precedes the spiritualization of the masses of humanity,

"If, therefore, the Most Great Peace is to follow the Lesser Peace, as it does follow, then the period for the full establishment and efflorescence of the Lesser Peace will not be a brief span of time, but a gradual process which will extend over a long period."

(Nakhjavání, 1984)

The Lesser Peace itself must evolve through various stages.

Referring to its initial stage, Mr. Nakhjavání recalled 'Abdu'l-Bahá and His response to a reporter for the *Montreal Star* —

"It will be established in this century. It will be universal in the twentieth century. All nations will be forced into it.

"It will be by general agreement. All the governments, 'Abdu'l-Bahá says, will disarm; and then He adds; they will disarm 'simultaneously.' "

(Nakhjavání, 1984 quoted from 'Abdu'l-Bahá in Canada, 35)

We will explore the nature of the inception of the Lesser Peace, as well as some of its stages in subsequent chapters.

AGES – PAST, PRESENT AND FUTURE

When the 'Most Great Peace' will be established is not exactly known, but it will occur in the Golden Age of the Bahá'í Dispensation. Within the Dispensation of Bahá'u'lláh there are three ages: the Heroic Age, the Formative Age, and the Golden Age. The Heroic Age commenced with the Declaration of the Báb in 1844 and closed with the passing of 'Abdu'l-Bahá in 1921. (GPB xiii) The Formative Age began in 1921 and will last until the Golden Age begins. The time of commencement of the Golden Age is not known but we do know that several objectives must be achieved before the Formative Age closes. (GPB 26) And we also know from the passage cited earlier from the Guardian in the foreward to God Passes By that the Golden Age and the Most Great Peace will emerge in the course of succeeding centuries within the Dispensation of Bahá'u'lláh. It is the present Age, the Formative Age, which we will examine next, to understand its purpose in light of the establishment of the Lesser Peace.

(See Table 3)

TABLE THREE

Ages of The Bahá'í Era

Heroic Age	1844-1921
Formative Age	1921-?
Golden Age	?-?

CHAPTER TWO

The Formative Age: The Age of Transition

THE INTEGRATING PROCESS

Now that we have examined some of the features which will characterize the future Most Great Peace, the ultimate goal towards which mankind is irresistibly moving, let us turn to the present age. We live now in the Formative Age, or the Age of Transition, which began in 1921. It is the —

> "Age in which the institutions, local, national, and international, of the Faith of Bahá'u'lláh were to take shape, develop and become fully consolidated, in anticipation of the third, the last, the Golden Age destined to witness the emergence of a world-embracing order enshrining the ultimate fruit of God's latest Revelation to mankind, a fruit whose maturity must signalize the establishment of a world civilization and the formal inauguration of the Kingdom of the Father upon earth as promised by Jesus Christ Himself."
>
> (GPB 324)

The Formative Age of the Bahá'í Era is witnessing —
> "the founding of the Administrative Order of the Faith of Bahá'u'lláh — a system which is at once the harbinger, the nucleus and pattern of His World Order."
>
> (GPB xv)

"The last twenty-three years of the first Bahá'í century may thus be regarded as the initial stage of the Formative Period of the Faith, an Age of Transition to be identified with the rise and establishment of the Administrative Order, upon which the institutions of the future Bahá'í Commonwealth must needs be ultimately erected in the Golden Age that must witness the consummation of the Bahá'í Dispensation. The Charter which called into being, outlined the features and set in motion the processes of, this Administrative Order is none other than the Will and Testament of 'Abdu'l-Bahá. His great legacy to posterity, the highest emanation of His mind and the mightiest instrument forged to ensure the continuity of the three ages which constitute the component parts of His Father's Dispensation."

(GPB 325)

"...The rise and establishment of the Administrative Order — the shell that shields and enshrines so precious a gem — constitutes the hallmark of this second and formative age of the Bahá'í Era. It will come to be regarded, as it recedes further and further from our eyes, the chief agency empowered to usher in the concluding phase, the consummation of this glorious Dispensation."

(WOB 156)

"The Administrative Order, which ever since 'Abdu'l-Bahá's ascension has evolved and is taking shape under our very eyes...may be considered as the framework of the Will itself, the inviolable stronghold wherein this new-born child is being nurtured and developed. This Administrative Order, as it expands and consolidates itself, will no doubt manifest the potentialities and reveal the full implications of this momentous Document — this most remarkable expression of the Will of One of the most remarkable Figures of the Dispensation of Bahá'u'lláh. It will, as its component parts, its organic institutions, begin to function with efficiency and vigor, assert its claim and demonstrate its capacity to be regarded not only as the nucleus but the very pattern of the new World Order destined to embrace in the fullness of time the whole of mankind."

(WOB 144)

It is clear from the above passages that the Formative period is characterized by building those institutions which will ultimately usher in the Most Great Peace, the Kingdom of God on Earth. This is the integrative and constructive process.

Some Objectives of the Formative Age

The beloved Guardian, though not indicating a date for the completion of the Formative Age, has specified objectives which must be achieved during this period, before humanity can move into the third age, the Golden Age.

"During this Formative Age of the Faith, and in the course of present and succeeding epochs, the last and crowning stage of the erection of the framework of the Administrative Order of the Faith of Bahá'u'lláh — the election of the Universal House of Justice — will have been completed, the Kitáb-i-Aqdas, the Mother

Book of His Revelation, will have been codified and its laws promulgated, the Lesser Peace will have been established, the unity of mankind will have been achieved and its maturity attained, the plan conceived by 'Abdu'l-Bahá will have been executed, the emancipation of the Faith from the fetters of religious orthodoxy will have been effected, and its independent religious status will have been universally recognized, whilst in the course of the Golden Age, destined to consummate the Dispensation itself, the banner of the Most Great Peace, promised by its Author, will have been unfurled, the World Bahá'í Commonwealth will have emerged in the plentitude of its power and splendor, and the birth and efflorescence of a world civilization, the child of that Peace, will have conferred its inestimable blessings upon all mankind."

(CF 6) (See Table 4)

TABLE FOUR

Formative Age

Objectives:

1. Universal House of Justice elected
2. Kitáb-i-Aqdas codified; laws promulgated
3. Lesser Peace established
4. Unity of mankind achieved
5. Maturity of mankind attained
6. Tablets of Divine Plan executed
7. Faith emancipated from fetters of religious orthodoxy
8. Independent status of Faith universally recognized

(CF 6)

Some of these objectives are associated directly with the development of the Bahá'í institutions, while others are to be achieved by the generality of mankind. The election of the Universal House of Justice was accomplished by the Bahá'ís of the world in 1963; the Kitáb-i-Aqdas was codified in 1973; the Divine Plan of 'Abdu'l-Bahá is in the process of execution on a global scale; the Faith is continually being recognized as an independent religion by an increasing number of governments in the world; and it is gradually being emancipated from the "fetters of religious orthodoxy." The establishment of the Lesser Peace will be inaugurated by the nations of the earth during the twentieth century. The unity and maturity of mankind will be a result of the interactive process between the generality of mankind and the influence of the Bahá'í teachings on mankind.

The Major and Minor Plans of God

The concept that the divine forces leading toward world unity are working in two different arenas, one within the Bahá'í community, the other amongst all mankind as a whole is explained by the beloved Guardian. The Universal House of Justice expounds upon this theme: —

> "We are told by Shoghi Effendi that two great processes are at work in the world: the great plan of God, tumultuous in its progress, working through mankind as a whole, tearing down barriers to world unity and forging humankind into a unified body in the fires of suffering and experience. This process will produce, in God's due time, the Lesser Peace, the political unification of the world. Mankind at that

time can be likened to a body that is unified but without life. The second process, the task of breathing life into the unified body — of creating true unity and spirituality culminating in the Most Great Peace — is that of the Bahá'í's who are laboring consciously, with detailed instructions and continuing divine guidance, to erect the fabric of the Kingdom of God on earth, into which they call their fellow men, thus conferring upon them eternal life.

"The working out of God's Major Plan proceeds mysteriously in ways directed by Him alone, but the Minor Plan that He has given us to execute, as our part in His grand design for the redemption of mankind, is clearly delineated. It is to this work that we must devote all our energies, for there is no one else to do it."

(WG 133-134) (See Tables 5 and 6)

TABLE FIVE

Plans of God

Major:
1. Works through mankind
2. Tears down barriers to unity
3. Forges humankind into a unified body (suffering/experience)
4. Produces the LESSER PEACE (political unification). Mankind is like a body unified but without life, at that time.

(WG 133-134)

Minor:

1. Fulfilled through Bahá'í Institutions
2. Divinely guided by:
   a. the Central Figures and the Guardian
   b. the Universal House of Justice
3. Bahá'ís breathe life into the body of mankind
4. Produces the Most Great Peace

(WG, 133-4)

THE DISINTEGRATING PROCESS

The second process associated with the Formative Age, the Age of Frustration, the Age of Transition, is the disintegrative process which will bring about momentous changes, upheavals and convulsions.

"...the latter [process], as its disintegrating influence deepens, tends to tear down, with increasing violence, the antiquated barriers that seek to block humanity's progress towards its destined goal. The constructive process stands associated with the nascent Faith of Bahá'u'lláh, and is the harbinger of the new World Order that Faith must erelong establish. The destructive forces that characterize the other should be identified with a civilization that has refused to answer to the expectation of a new age, and is consequently falling into chaos and decline.

"A titanic, a spiritual struggle, unparalleled in its magnitude yet unspeakably glorious in its ultimate consequences, is being waged as a result of these opposing tendencies, in this age of transition through which the organized community of the followers of Bahá'u'lláh and mankind as a whole are passing."

(WOB 170)

From Adolescence to Maturity

In this transitional age we observe

"...manifold evidences of that universal fermentation which, in every continent of the globe and in every department of human life, be it religious, social, economic, or political, is purging and reshaping humanity in anticipation of the Day when the wholeness of the human race will have been recognized and its unity established."

(WOB 170)

Every adjustment that is required to advance from adolescence into adulthood must be made during this period of Transition.

"What we witness at the present time, during 'this gravest crises in the history of civilization,'...is the adolescent stage in the slow and painful evolution of humanity, preparatory to the attainment of the stage of manhood, the stage of maturity, the promise of which is embedded in the teachings, and enshrined in the prophecies of Bahá'u'lláh. The tumult of this age of transition is characteristic of the impetuosity and irrational instincts of youth, its follies, its prodigality, its pride, its self-assurance, its rebelliousness, and contempt of discipline.

"The ages of its infancy and childhood are past, never again to return, while the Great Age, the consummation of all ages, which must signalize the coming of age of the entire human race is yet to come. The convulsions of this transitional and most turbulent period in the annals of humanity are the essential prerequisites, and herald the inevitable approach, of that Age of Ages, 'the time of the end,' in which the folly and tumult of strife that has, since the dawn of history, blackened the annals of mankind, will have been finally transmuted into the wisdom and the tranquility of an undisturbed, a universal, and lasting peace, in which the discord and separation of the children of men will have given way to the worldwide reconciliation, and the complete unification of the diverse elements that constitute human society."

(PDC 117)

An Age of Travail

The age of Transition is characterized by the Guardian as a period whose —

"...tribulations are the precursors of that Era of blissful felicity which is to incarnate God's ultimate purpose for all mankind."

(WOB 171)

It is

"...a period of intense turmoil and wide-spread suffering...overshadowed by such moral and social gloom as can alone prepare an unrepentant humanity for the prize she is destined to inherit."

(WOB 168)

"Into such a period we are now steadily and irresistibly moving. Amidst the shadows which are increasingly gathering about us we can faintly discover the glimmerings of Bahá'u'lláh's unearthly sovereignty appearing fitfully on the horizon of history. To us, the 'generation of the half-light,' living at a time which may be designated as the period of incubation of the World Commonwealth envisaged by Bahá'u'lláh, has been assigned a task whose high privilege we can never sufficiently appreciate, and the arduousness of which we can as yet but dimly recognize. We may well believe, we who are called upon to experience the operation of the dark forces destined to unloose a flood of agonizing afflictions, that the darkest hour that must precede the dawn of the Golden Age of our Faith has not yet struck. Deep as is the gloom that already encircles the world, the afflictive ordeals which that world is to suffer are still in preparation, nor can their blackness be as yet imagined. We stand on the threshold of an age whose convulsions proclaim alike the death-pangs of the old order and the birth-pangs of the new. Through the generating influence of the Faith announced by Bahá'u'lláh this New World Order may be said to have been conceived. We can, at the present moment, experience its stirrings in the womb of a travailing age — an age waiting for the appointed hour at which it can cast its burden and yield its fairest fruit."

(WOB 168-169)

"The process of disintegration must inexorably continue, and its corrosive influence must penetrate deeper and deeper into the very core of a crumbling age. Much suffering will still be required ere the contending nations, creeds, classes and races of mankind are fused in the crucible of universal affliction, and are forged by the fires of a fierce ordeal into one organic commonwealth, one vast, unified and harmoniously functioning system. Adversities unimaginably appalling, undreamed of crisis and upheavals, war, famine, and pestilence, might well combine to engrave in the soul of an unheeding generation those truths and principles which it has disdained to recognize and follow. A paralysis more painful than any it has yet experienced must creep over and further afflict the fabric of a broken society ere it can be rebuilt and regenerated."

(WOB 193-194)

"Adversity, prolonged, worldwide, afflictive, allied to chaos and universal destruction, must needs convulse the nations, stir the conscience of the world, disillusion the masses, precipitate a radical change in the very conception of society, and coalesce ultimately the disjointed, the bleeding limbs of mankind into one body, single, organically united and indivisible."

(PDC 122-123)

THE FRUITS OF SUFFERING

You may be asking yourself at this point, "Why do we have to suffer so much before universal peace can be attained?" We have only to turn to the Writings to find several reasons for such suffering —

> "O Son of Man!
> My calamity is my providence, outwardly it is fire and vengeance, but inwardly it is light and mercy. Hasten thereunto that thou mayest become an eternal light and an immortal spirit. This is my command unto thee, do thou observe it."
>
> (AHW no. 51)

"We have but to turn our gaze to humanity's blood-stained history to realize that nothing short of intense mental as well as physical agony has been able to precipitate those epoch-making changes that constitute the greatest landmarks in the history of human civilization."

(WOB 45)

"Great and far-reaching as have been those changes in the past, they cannot appear, when viewed in their proper perspective, except as a subsidiary adjustments preluding that transformation of unparalleled majesty and scope which humanity is in this age bound to undergo. That the forces of a world catastrophe can alone precipitate such a new phase of human thought is, alas, becoming increasingly apparently. Nothing short of the fire of a severe ordeal, unparalleled in its intensity, can fuse and weld the discordant entities that constitute the elements of present day civilization into the integral components of the world commonwealth of the future, is a truth which future events will increasingly demonstrate.

"The prophetic voice of Bahá'u'lláh's warning, in the concluding passages of the Hidden Words, to 'the peoples of the world' that 'an unforeseen calamity is following them and that grievous retribution awaiteth them' throws indeed a lurid light upon the immediate fortunes of sorrowing humanity. Nothing but a fiery ordeal, out of which humanity will emerge, chastened and, prepared, can succeed in implanting that sense of responsibility which the leaders of a new-born age must arise to shoulder."

(WOB 46)

It seems that ordinary means of effecting a change in the minds of the leaders of the world are inadequate. For them to willingly cede some of their own sovereignty to an international federation of nations, for them to put aside national and racial prejudices, for them to share whatever natural resources they have within their borders with the rest of the world — for all these major changes to occur, ordinary means of diplomacy, negotiations, pleading, or calculating are not capable of bringing about the radical changes required to establish a just system of Order.

"Dearly-beloved friends! Humanity, whether viewed in the light of man's individual conduct or in the existing relationships between organized communities and nations, has, alas, strayed too far and suffered too great a decline to be redeemed through the unaided efforts of the best among its recognized rulers and statesmen — however disinterested their motives, however concerted their action, however unsparing their zeal and devotion to its cause. No scheme which the calculations of the highest statesmanship may yet devise; no doctrine which the most distinguished exponents of economic theory may strive to inculcate, can provide, in the last resort, adequate foundations upon which the future of a distracted world can be built..."

(WOB 34)

The Hand of the Cause of God Amatu'l-Bahá Rúhíyyih Khánúm, the wife of the Guardian, put it quite aptly —
"If we, the generation of the twilight before the sun of this new day rises, ask ourselves why such catastrophes should be facing us in these times, the answers are all there, made crystal clear by the Guardian in his great expositions of the meaning and implications of our teachings. Two factors, he taught us, are involved. The first is contained in those words of Bahá'u'lláh, 'Soon will the present-day order be

rolled up, and a new one spread out in its stead.' To tear off the time-honored protective covering of innumerable societies, each embedded in its own customs, superstitions and prejudices, and apply to them a universal new frame of existence is an operation only Almighty God can perform and of necessity a very painful one. This made even more painful by the state of men's souls and minds; some societies are the victims of 'a flagrant secularism the direct offspring of irreligion,' some are in the grip of 'a blatant materialism and racialism' which have, Shoghi Effendi stated, 'usurped the rights of God Himself,' but all the peoples of the earth are guilty of having for over a century, 'refused to recognize the One Whose advent has been promised to all religions, and in Whose Faith alone, all nations can and must eventually seek their true salvation! Fundamentally it was because of this new Faith, this 'priceless gem of Divine Revelation enshrining the Spirit of God and incarnating His Purpose for all mankind in this age' as Shoghi Effendi described it, that the world was 'undergoing such agonies.' Bahá'u'lláh Himself had said: 'The world's equilibrium hath been upset through the vibrating influence of this most great, this new World Order.' 'The signs of impending convulsions and chaos can now be discerned, inasmuch as the prevailing Order appeareth to be lamentably defective.' 'The world is in travail and its agitation waxeth day by day. Its face is turned towards waywardness and unbelief. Such shall be its plight that to disclose it now would not be meet and seemly. Its perversity will long continue and when the appointed hour is come, there shall suddenly appear

The Formative Age : The Age of Transition   43

that which shall cause the limbs of mankind to quake. Then and only then will the Divine Standard be unfurled and the Nightingale of Paradise warble its melody.' 'After a time, all the governments on earth will change. Oppression will envelop the world. And following a universal convulsion, the Sun of justice will rise from the horizon of the unseen realm.'

"So thrilling, however, is the vision of the future which Shoghi Effendi painted for us in his brilliant words, that it wipes away all fear and fills the heart of every Bahá'í with such confidence and joy that the prospect of any amount of suffering and deprivation cannot weaken his Faith or crush his hopes. 'The world is the truth,' Shoghi Effendi wrote, 'moving on towards its destiny. The interdependence of the peoples and nations of the earth, whatever the leaders of the devisive forces of the world may say or do, is already an accomplished fact.' The world commonwealth, 'destined to emerge, sooner or later, out of the carnage, agony, and havoc of this great world convulsion' was the assured consummation of the working of these forces."

(PP 194-195)

The purpose of suffering is to purify the heart and mind from those ideas which prevent us from drawing closer to God and to one another. This can be clearly seen in the expectant mother who gives the strength of her body and thoughts to the new life stirring within her. She must take special measures to ensure that her diet and lifestyle promote the nurturing of that new life. Often, she must sacrifice foods, activities, and pursuits during her pregnancy to ensure that her body will receive the necessary rest required to support her baby. The baby's system will first be nurtured from the vital life support system of the mother. The mother will be sustained by whatever is not utilized by the growing fetus. As she anticipates the birth, she may learn from older women, or from modern childbirth classes, what to expect. She prepares her mind, body and spirit for the momentous event. Perhaps she will prepare by learning exercises to reduce the pain of contractions, to relax the body during labor, to systematically train her body to accept the flow of the contractions, rather than aggravating the situation by becoming more tense — a reaction quite common amongst mothers who have not learned what to expect.

The Bahá'í community, knowledgeable about the upcoming "convulsions" and "world upheavals," can be prepared for this "age of travail" if we have carefully familiarized ourselves with the sacred Writings on the nature of the Age of Transition. The generality of mankind neither clearly understands what is happening in our times, nor why. They do not have the assurance that the world is headed towards peace. Their worst fears concern the ultimate annihilation of vast segments, if not all, of humanity. We, on the other hand, have the promises that —

> "My calamity is My providence, outwardly it is fire and vengeance, and inwardly, it is light and mercy..."
>
> (AHW no. 51)

We do not believe that the destructive forces unleashed in this age are leading to the literal end of the world, but rather that these forces are purging mankind in preparation for a New Order.

> "The whole earth is now in a state of pregnancy. The day is approaching when it will have yielded its

noblest fruits, when from it will have sprung forth the loftiest trees, the most enchanting blossoms, the most heavenly blessings..."

(WOB 169)

The Need for Spiritual Midwives

Just as it is not uncommon for women who are uneducated to be ignorant of the signs and symptoms of pregnancy, and some even arrive at the point of labor not knowing they are pregnant, it is also not uncommon for the masses of humanity to be unaware of the new life which is presently stirring in the womb of this travailing age. It is at the critical point of labor and childbirth that the expectant mother needs a helper, such as, a doctor or a midwife. The Bahá'ís of the world, living in small villages and communities everywhere, knowing the signs of this age and fully conscious of the fruit which is to be plucked after a period of intense global afflictions, can assist their fellowmen to anticipate the new infant of the twentieth century, the Lesser Peace. We can serve as spiritual midwives to a travailing humanity at a time when the ordeals appear to have neither purpose nor end. We can offer comfort to those who are in pain, anguish, and utter confusion about the cause of and necessity for worldwide upheavals.

After humanity casts her burden, the new life which was stirring within her during this state of pregnancy, this Age of Transition, will be welcomed with open arms. The child we will see at first will be the Lesser Peace, which the nations of the earth, as yet unconscious of Bahá'u'lláh's Revelation, will themselves establish. That child is destined to grow and develop until its maturity in the emergence of the Most Great Peace.

CHAPTER THREE

Outstanding Events of the Formative Age

"LET THEM BE SWEPT AWAY"

"Those who care for the future of the human race may well ponder this advice. 'If long-cherished ideals and time-honored institutions, if certain social assumptions and religious formulae have ceased to promote the welfare of the generality of mankind, if they no longer minister to the needs of a continually evolving humanity, let them be swept away and relegated to the limbo of obsolescent and forgotten doctrines. Why should these, in a world subject to the immutable law of change decay, be exempt from the deterioration that must needs overtake every human institution? For legal standards, political and economic theories are solely designed to safeguard the interests of humanity as a whole, and not humanity to be crucified for the preservation of the integrity of any particular law or doctrine.''

(PWP 5)

The Collapse of Empires

Shoghi Effendi devotes the bulk of his book ***The Promised Day Is Come*** to a detailed analysis of the "titanic upheavals" which are relentlessly gripping the World in the Formative Age. Their source, their direction, their necessity and their consummation are fully explained to us in order that we can play our vital part in this intense drama.

To illustrate the point, I list the major events that have already taken place during this Age of Transition. The two earliest events which occurred were the —

"...dissolution of the German Empire, the humiliating defeat inflicted upon its ruler, the successor and lineal descendant of the Prussian King and Emperor to whom Bahá'u'lláh had addressed His solemn and historic warning, together with the extinction of the Austro-Hungarian Monarchy, the remnant of the once-great Holy Roman Empire, were both precipitated by a war whose outbreak signalized the opening of the Age of Frustration [Formative Age] destined to precede the establishment of the World Order of Bahá'u'lláh.

(WOB 171)

The Decline of Islám

"The collapse of the power of Shí'ih hierarchy, in a land which had for centuries been one of the impregnable strongholds of Muslim fanaticism, was the inevitable consequence of that wave of secularization which, at a later time, was to invade some of the most powerful and conservative ecclesiastical institutions in both the European and American continents. Though not the direct outcome of the last war, this sudden trembling which had seized this hitherto immovable pillar of Islamic orthodoxy accentuated the problems and deepened the restlessness with which a war-weary world was being afflicted. Shí'ih Islám had lost once for all, in Bahá'u'lláh's native land and as the direct consequence of its implacable hostility to His Faith, its combative power, had forfeited its rights and privileges, had been degraded and demoralized, and was being condemned to hopeless obscurity and extinction."

(WOB 172)

"The downfall of the Qájár dynasty, the avowed defender and the willing instrument of a decaying clergy, almost synchronized with the humiliation which the Shí'ih ecclesiastical leaders had suffered. From Muḥammad Sháh down to the last and feeble monarch of that dynasty, the Faith of Bahá'u'lláh was denied the impartial consideration, the disinterested and fair treatment which its cause had rightly demanded. It had, on the contrary, been atrociously harassed, consistently betrayed and prosecuted. ...One more barrier that had sought to obstruct the forward march of the Faith was now removed."

(WOB 173)

"...The overthrow of the Sultanate and the Caliphate, the twin pillars of Súnní Islám, can be regarded in no other light except as the inevitable consequence of the fierce, the sustained and deliberate persecution..."

(WOB 173)

against the Cause of Bahá'u'lláh.
"...From the time Bahá'u'lláh set foot on Turkish soil and was made a virtual prisoner of the most powerful potentate of Islam to the year of the Holy Land's liberation from Turkish yoke, successive Caliphs, and in particular the Sultans 'Abdu'l-Azíz and 'Abdu'l-Ḥamíd, had, in full exercise of the spiritual and temporal authority which their exalted office had conferred upon them, afflicted both the founder of

our Faith and the Center of His Covenant with such pain and tribulation as no mind can fathom nor Pen or tongue describe."

(WOB 174)

As a result, the following internal convulsions seized the Turkish Empire and struck down the Sultanate and the Caliphate: —

"...the murder of that arrogant despot in the year 1876; the Russo-Turkish conflict that soon followed in its wake; the wars of liberation which succeeded it; the rise of the Young Turk movement; the Turkish Revolution of 1909 that precipitated the downfall of 'Abdu'l-Hamíd; the Balkan wars with their calamitous consequences; the liberation of Palestine...; the further dismemberment of the Treaty of Versailles; the abolition of the Sultanate and the downfall of the House of Uthman; the extinction of the Caliphate; the disestablishment of the State Religion; the annulment of Sharíáh Law and the promulgation of a universal Civil code; the suppression of various orders, beliefs, traditions and ceremonials believed to be inextricably interwoven with the fabric of the Muslim Faith these followed with an ease and swiftness that no man had dared envisage."

(WOB 175)

"If I have dwelt too long on this theme, if I have to a disproportionate degree, quoted from the sacred Writings in support of my argument, it is solely because of my firm conviction that these retributive calamities that have rained down upon the foremost oppressor of the Faith of Bahá'u'lláh should rank not only among the stirring occurrences of this Age of

Transition, but as some of the startling and significant events of contemporary history."

(WOB 179-180)

The Deterioration of Christian Institutions

To Christianity the Age of Transition has posed new threats to its survival that it has never before experienced.

"Forces of irreligion, of a purely materialistic philosophy, of unconcealed paganism have been unloosed, are now spreading, and by consolidating themselves, are beginning to invade some of the most powerful Christian institutions of the western world..."

(WOB 180)

"This menace of secularism...has already manifested itself in both Europe and American, and is, in varying degrees, and under various forms and designations, challenging the basis of every established religion, and in particular the institutions and communities identified with the Faith of Jesus Christ. ...'But to the Church overseas these things are grim realities, enemies with which it is at grips...The Church has a new danger to face in land after land — determined and hostile attack. From Soviet Russia a definitely anti-religious Communism is pushing west into Europe and America, East into Persia, India, China and Japan. It is an economic theory, definitely harnessed to a disbelief in God. It is a religious irreligion...' Equally deliberate in some lands in its determined hostility to Christianity is another form of social and political faith — nationalism."

(WQB 181-182)

"The excessive growth of industrialism and its attendant evils — as the aforementioned quotation bears witness — the aggressive policies initiated and the persistent efforts exerted by the inspirers and organizers of the Communist movement; the intensification of a militant nationalism, associated in certain countries with a systematized work of defamation against all forms of ecclesiastical influence, have no doubt contributed to the de-Christianization of the masses, and been responsible for a notable decline in the authority, the prestige and power of the Church."

(WOB 182)

"The disestablishment and dismemberment of the Greek Orthodox Church in Russia, following upon the blow which the church of Rome had sustained as a result of the collapse of the Austro-Hungarian Monarchy; the commotion that subsequently seized the Catholic Church and culminated in its separation from the State of Islam; the persecution of that same Church of Mexico; the perquisitions, arrests, intimidation and terrorization to which Catholics and Lutherans alike are being subjected in the heart of Europe; the turmoil into which another branch of the Church has been thrown as a result of the military campaign in Africa; the decline that has set in the fortunes of Christian Missions, both Anglican and Presbyterian, in Persia, Turkey, and the Far East; the ominous signs that foreshadow serious complications in the equivocal and precarious relationships now existing between the Holy See and certain nations in the continent of Europe — these stand out as the most striking features of the reverses which, in almost every part of the world, the members and leaders of Christian ecclesiastical institutions have suffered."

(WOB 183)

Christian —
"institutions as have strayed far from the spirit and teachings of Jesus Christ must of necessity, as the embryonic World Order of Bahá'u'lláh takes shape and unfolds, recede into the background, and make way for the progress of the divinely-ordained institutions that stand inextricably interwoven with His teachings."

(WOB 185)

Signs of Moral Downfall

The disintegration of religious institutions,
"...constitutes so important an aspect of the Formative Period of the Bahá'í Era. ...Its counterpart can also be found in the life and conduct of the individuals that compose them."

(WOB 186)

"No wonder, therefore, that when, as a result of human perversity, the light of religion is quenched in men's hearts, and the divinely appointed Robe, designed to adorn the human temple, is deliberately discarded, a deplorable decline in the fortunes of humanity immediately sets in, bringing in its wake all the evils which a wayward soul is capable of revealing. The perversion of human nature, the degradation of human conduct, the conception and dissolution of human institutions, reveal themselves, under such circumstances, in their worst and most revolting aspects. Human character is debased, confidence is shaken, the nerves of discipline are relaxed, the voice of human conscience is stilled, the sense of decency and shame is obscured, conceptions of duty, of solidarity, of reciprocity and loyalty are distorted, and the very feeling of peacefulness, joy and of hope is gradually extinguished...Such...is the state which individuals and institutions alike are approaching..."

"The recrudescence of religious intolerance, of racial animosity, and of patriotic arrogance; the increasing evidences of selfishness, of suspicion, of fear and of fraud; the spread of terrorism, of lawlessness, of drunkenness and of crime; the unquenchable thirst for, and the feverish pursuit after, earthly vanities, riches and pleasures; the weakening of family solidarity; the laxity in parental control; the lapse into luxurious indulgence; the irresponsible attitude towards marriage and the consequent rising tide of divorce; the degeneracy of art and music, the infection of literature, and the corruption of the press; the extension of the influence and activities of those 'prophets of decadence' who advocate companionate marriage, who preach the philosophy of nudism, who call modesty an intellectual fiction, who refuse to regard the procreation of children as the sacred and primary purpose of marriage, who denounce religion as an opiate of the people, who would, if given full reign, lead back the human race to barbarism, chaos, and ultimate extinction — these appear as the outstanding characteristics of a decadent society, a society that must either be reborn or perish."

(WOB 187-188)

The Breakdown of Political and Economic Structure

Regarding the breakdown of political and economic structures, Shoghi Effendi said in 1936 —
"...The disastrous failure of both the Disarmament and Economic Conferences; the obstacles confronting the negotiations for the limitation of naval armaments; the withdrawal of two of the most powerful and heavily armed nations of the world from the activities and membership of the League of Nations; the ineptitude of the parliamentary system of government as witnessed by the recent developments in Europe and America; the inability of the leaders and exponents of the Communist Movement to vindicate the much-vaunted principle of the Dictatorship of the Proletariat; the perils and privations to which the rulers of the Totalitarian states have, in recent years, exposed their subjects — all these demonstrate, beyond the shadow of a doubt, the impotence of present-day institutions to avert the calamities with which human society is being increasingly threatened. What else remains, a bewildered generation may well ask, that can repair the cleavage that is constantly widening, and which may, at any time, engulf it?"

(WOB 189-190)

All of these momentous events associated with the disintegrating forces unleashed in the Age of Transition are —
"...Strangely reminiscent of the Fall of the Roman Empire in the West, which threatens to engulf the whole structure of present-day civilization — all witness the tumult which the birth of this mighty Organ

of the Religion of Bahá'u'lláh has cast into the world — a tumult which will grow in scope and in intensity as the implications of this constantly evolving Scheme are more fully understood and its ramifications more widely extended over the surface of the globe."

(WOB 156)

Again, the parallel between the world in travail and the expectant mother seems appropriate. Once the new being is conceived in the womb of the mother, its gradual development necessitates that all the vital internal organs near, or surrounding the new being move over, adjust to, and modify their shape in deference to the growing child. This new being cannot be ignored.

All the systems of the planet, be they economic, political, religious, or social must make way and adjust to the new forms that Bahá'u'lláh has created in the midmost heart of the earth. All past systems must be transformed or perish. The new forms of institutions are fully suited to meet the needs of a globe which is crying out for its unification. The old earth must change the scope, shape and features of its old institutions into the world-encircling, all-inclusive, new shapes and forms conceived by Bahá'u'lláh.

One thing is definite — once new life is conceived and growing within the expectant mother, her shape definitely undergoes remarkable changes. Though the period of pregnancy causes accompanying changes in hormones, weight, blood pressure, pulse, etc., once the newborn arrives, the mother gradually regains a state of equilibrium, although it seems, not the same as before the pregnancy. A new state of equilibrium is attained, and having been through the experience of ushering in new life, she is more mature. And if she has been preparing conscientiously for her child, she is ready to provide it with loving nurture.

So shall it be for the Bahá'ís who have been diligently preparing for and sacrificing for the coming of age of humanity destined to be attained in this, the Age of Transition.

WARS – CAUSES AND CONSEQUENCES

The primary cause of world unrest in this century has been the failure of the world's recognized leaders "...to adjust these systems of economic and political institutions to the imperative needs of a rapidly evolving age..." Wars, then, are "...intermittent crises that convulse present-day society..." and are due primarily to –

> "the lamentable inability of the world's recognized leaders to read aright the signs of the times, to rid themselves once for all of their preconceived ideas and fettering creeds, and to reshape the machinery of their respective governments according to those standards that are implicit in Bahá'u'lláh's supreme declaration of the Oneness of Mankind."
>
> (WOB 36)

World War I

The general cause of wars in this age has been mentioned above. Let us turn to the consequences of the great World Wars in this Age of Frustration –

> "How poignantly some of us can recall His ['Abdu'l-Bahá's] pregnant remarks, in the presence of the pilgrims and visitors who thronged His doors on the

morrow of the jubilant celebrations and greeted the termination of the World War — a war which by the horrors it evoked, the losses it entailed and the complications it engendered, was destined to exert so far-reaching an influence on the fortunes of mankind. How serenely, yet powerfully, He stressed the cruel deception which a Pact, hailed by the peoples and nations as the embodiment of triumphant justice and the unfailing instrument of an abiding peace, held in store for an unrepentant humanity. 'Peace, Peace,' how often we heard Him remark, 'the lips of potentates and peoples increasingly proclaim, whereas the fire of unquenched hatreds still smoulders in their hearts.' How often we heard Him raise His voice, whilst the tumult of triumphant enthusiasm was still at its height and long before the faintest misgivings could have been felt or expressed, confidently declaring that the Document, extolled as the Charter of a liberated humanity, contained within it seeds of such bitter deception as would further enslave the world. How abundant are now the evidences that attest the perspicacity of His unerring judgment.
"Ten years of unceasing turmoil, so laden with anguish, so fraught with incalculable consequences to the future of civilization, have brought the world to the verge of a calamity too awful to contemplate. Sad indeed is the contrast between the manifestations of confident enthusiasm in which the Plenipotentiaries at Versailles so fully indulged and the cry of unconcealed distress which victors and vanquished alike are now raising in the hour of bitter delusion."

(WOB 29-30)

"The disquieting influence of over thirty million souls living under minority conditions throughout the continent of Europe; the vast and ever-swelling army of the unemployed with its crushing burden and demoralizing influence on governments and peoples; the wicked, unbridled race of armaments swallowing an ever-increasing share of the substance of already impoverished nations; the utter demoralization from which the international financial markets are now increasingly suffering; the onslaught of secularism invading what has hitherto been regarded as the impregnably strongholds of Christian and Muslim Orthodoxy — these stand out as the gravest symptoms that bode ill for the future stability of the structure of modern civilization...

"Might we not already discern, as we scan the political horizon, the alignment of those forces that are dividing afresh the continent of Europe into camps of potential combatants, determined upon a contest that may, unlike the last war, the end of an epoch, a vast epoch, in the history of human evolution? Are we, the privileged custodians of a priceless Faith, called upon to witness a cataclysmical change, politically as fundamental and spiritually as beneficent as that which precipitated the fall of the Roman Empire in the West? Might it not happen — every vigilant adherent of the Faith of Bahá'u'lláh might well pause to reflect — that out of this world eruption there may stream forces of such spiritual energy as shall recall, nay eclipse, the splendor of those signs and wonders that accompanied the establishment of the Faith of Jesus Christ?"

(WOB 32-33)

The League of Nations

Within the background of general world convulsions, the golden thread of a slowly-evolving movement towards World Peace can be detected. One of the constructive outcomes of World War I was the founding of the League of Nations. During World War I America was thrown into "the vortex of the first stage of a world upheaval." To President Woodrow Wilson —

"...must be ascribed the unique honor, among all statesmen of any nation, whether of the East or of the West, of having voiced sentiments so akin to the principles of the Cause of Bahá'u'lláh, and of having more than any other world leader, contributed to the creation of the League of Nations — achievements which the pen of the Center of God's Covenant acclaimed as signalizing the dawn of the Most Great Peace, whose sun, according to that same pen must needs arise as the direct consequence of the enforcement of the laws of the dispensation of Bahá'u'lláh."

(CF 36)

"Would it be untrue to maintain that in a world of steadily mounting armaments, of unquenchable hatreds and rivalries, the progress, however fitful of the forces marking in harmony with the spirit of the age can already be discerned? Though the great outcry raised by post-war [World War I] nationalism is growing louder and more insistent every day, the League of Nations is as yet in its embryonic state, and the storm clouds that are gathering may for a time totally eclipse its powers and obliterate its machinery, yet the direction in which the institution itself is operating is most significant. The voices that have been raised ever since its inception, the efforts that have been exerted, the work that has already been accomplished, foreshadow the triumphs which this presently constituted institution, or any other body that may supercede it, is destined to achieve."

(WOB 191)

The conclusion of World War I —
"...gave birth to the institution of the League of Nations, the precursor of that World Tribunal which, as prophesied by..."
Bahá'u'lláh —
"...the peoples and nations of the earth must needs unitedly establish."

(GPB 305)

"The League of Nations, its opponents will observe, still lacks the universality which is the prerequisite of abiding success in the efficacious settlement of international disputes. The United States of America, its begetter, has repudiated it, and is still holding aloof, while Germany and Japan, who ranked among its most powerful supporters, have abandoned its cause and withdrawn from its membership. The decisions arrived at and the action thus far taken, others will maintain, should be regarded as no more than a magnificent gesture, rather than a conclusive evidence of international solidarity. Still others may contend that though such a verdict has been pronounced, and such pledges been given, collective action must, in the end, fail in its ultimate purpose, and that the League itself will perish and be submerged by the flood of tribulations destined to overtake the whole race. Be that as it may, the significance of the steps already taken cannot be ignored. Whatever the present status of the League on the outcome of its historic verdict, whatever the trials and reverses which, in the immediate future, it may have to face and sustain, the fact must be recognized that so important a decision marks one of the most distinctive milestones on the long and arduous road that must lead it to its goal, the stage at which the oneness of the whole body of nations will be made the ruling principle of international life."

(WOB 193)

"That no less than fifty nations, should have, after mature deliberation, recognized and been led to pronounce their verdict against an act of aggression which in their judgment has been deliberately committed by one of their fellow-members, one of the foremost Powers of Europe; that they should have, for the most part, agreed to impose collectively sanctions on the condemned aggressor, and should have succeeded in carrying out, to a very great measure, their decision, is no doubt an event without parallel in human history. For the first time in the history of humanity the system of collective security, foreshadowed by Bahá'u'lláh and explained by 'Abdu'l-Bahá, has been seriously envisaged, discussed and tested... For the first time in human history tentative efforts have been exerted by the nations of the world to assume collective responsibility, and to supplement their verbal pledges by actual preparation for collective action..."

(WOB 191-192)

World War II

After World War I,
> " 'Abdu'l-Bahá asserted in unequivocal language that 'another war, fiercer than the last will assuredly break out...' "

(WOB 46)

'Abdu'l-Bahá, in a Tablet written soon after World War I,
> "...anticipates, in succinct and ominous sentences, the successive ebullitions which must afflict humanity, and whose full force the American nation must, if her destiny is to be accomplished, inevitably experience. 'The ills from which the world now suffers...will multiply; the gloom which envelopes it will deepen. The Balkans will remain discontented. Its restlessness will increase. The vanquished powers will continue to agitate. They will resort to every measure that may rekindle the flame of war. Movements, newly born and world-wide in their range, will exert their utmost effort for the advancement of their designs. The movement of the Left will acquire great importance. Its influence will spread.'

> "The agitation in the Balkan Peninsula; the feverish activity which Germany and Italy played a disastrous role, culminating in the outbreak of the second World War; the rise of the Fascist and Nazi movements, which spread their ramification to distant parts of the globe; the spread of communism which, as a result of the victory of Soviet Russia in that same war, has been greatly accelerated — all these happenings, some unequivocally, others in veiled language, have been forecast in the Tablet, the full force of whose implications are as yet undisclosed, and

which, we may well anticipate, the American nation, as yet insufficiently schooled by adversity, must sooner or later experience."

(CF 37)

"Though Shoghi Effendi saw another war coming, he did not live in a constant state of false emergency. He reassured Martha Root, who in 1927 wrote to him from Erope about her fears: 'As to the matter of an eventual war that may break out in Europe, do not feel in the least concerned or worried. The prospect is very remote, the danger for the near future is non-existent' — even though that same year he had stated that the inevitability of another deadly conflict was becoming increasingly manifest. Over and over he prepared the minds of the Bahá'í's to face the fact that a world conflagration was coming. In 1938 he wrote: 'The twin processes of internal disintegration and external chaos are being accelerated and every day are inexorably moving towards a climax. The rumblings that must precede the eruption of those forces that must cause "the limbs of mankind to quake" can already be heard. "The time of the end," "the latter years," as foretold in the Scriptures, are at long last upon us.'..."

On the 30th of August 1939 he cabled —
" '...shades night descending imperilled humanity inexorably deepening...' ...July 1940 he cabled via Haifa that the fires of war '...now threaten devastation both Near East Far West respectively enshrining World Centre chief remaining citadel Faith Bahá'u'lláh...' "

(PP 181-182)

In 1941 the Guardian wrote the *Promised Day is Come* in which he indicated the significance of World War II, the darkness of the immediate future, and the glorious radiance of the distant future.

> " 'The convulsions of this transitional and most turbulent period in the annals of humanity are the essential prerequisites, and herald the inevitable approach, of that Age of Ages, "the time of the end," in which the folly and tumult of strife that has since the dawn of history, blackened the annals of mankind, will have been finally transmuted into the wisdom and tranquility of an undisturbed, a universal, and lasting peace... It is for this stage that this vast, this fiery ordeal which humanity is experiencing is mysteriously paving the way.' "
>
> (PP 185)

One of the positive consequences of America entering World War II is that she —

> "...redressed the balance, saved mankind the horrors of devastation and bloodshed involved in the prolongation of hostilities, and decisively contributed...to the overthrow of the exponents of ideologies fundamentally at variance with the universal tenets of our Faith."
>
> (CF 36)

The United Nations

Another consequence was

> "the splendid initiative taken, ...by the American Government, culminating in the birth of the successor of that League in San Francisco [United Nations], and the establishment of its permanent seat in the city of New York."
>
> (CF 36)

It is of interest to note that the beloved Guardian forged links between the International Bahá'í Community and the United Nations. He guided and directed the eventual recognition of the independent status of the Bahá'í Faith as a non-government organization entitled to representation to the United Nations. This enhanced the prestige of the Faith and "increased the privileges of the official Bahá'í representatives who regularly attended and took part in United Nations conferences of any type open to those enjoying such status."

(PP 304)

Until the end of his life Shoghi Effendi strengthened the ties between the Bahá'í Faith and the United Nations and this relationship has continued to be fostered by the Universal House of Justice.

"The importance Shoghi Effendi attached to this tie linking the Cause with the greatest international instrument ever forged in human history is reflected in his own words: 'It marks an important step forward in the struggle of our beloved Faith to receive in the eyes of the world its just due, and to be recognized as an independent World Religion. Indeed, this step should have a favourable reaction on the progress of the Cause everywhere, especially in those parts of the world where it is still persecuted, belittled, or scorned, particularly in the East.' "

(PP 304)

Post World War II

"In post-war years, as the victories the Bahá'í's were winning multiplied and the United Nations — the mightiest instrument for creating peace that men had ever devised — emerged, many of us no doubt hoped, and wishfully believed, that we had left the worst phase of humanity's long history of war behind us and that we could now discover the first light of that dawn the Bahá'í's are so firmly convinced lies ahead for the world. But the sober, guided mind of the Guardian did not see events in this light. Until the end of his life he continued to make the same remark, based on Bahá'u'lláh's own words, that He had so often made before the war: 'The distant future is very bright, but the immediate future is very dark.' "

(PP 189-190)

In 1947 in a message to the American Bahá'í community he wrote —

" 'As the international situation worsens, as the fortunes of mankind sink to a still lower ebb...as the fabric of present-day society heaves and cracks under the strain and stress of portentous events and calamities, as the fissures, accentuating the cleavage separating nation from nation, class from class, race from race, and creed from creed multiply...' "

"In November of that same year...he wrote: 'As the threat of still more violent convulsions assailing a travailing age increases, and the wings of yet another conflict, destined to contribute a distinct, and perhaps a decisive, share to the birth of the new Order which must signalize the advent of the Lesser Peace, darken the international horizon...' 'The deepening crisis ominously threatening further to derange the equilibrium of a politically convulsed, economically disrupted, socially subverted, morally decadent and spiritually moribund society.' He went on to speak of the 'premonitory rumblings of a third ordeal threatening to engulf the Eastern and Western Hemispheres' and said 'the world outlook is steadily darkening.' He urged the Bahá'í's to 'forge ahead into the future serenely confident that the hour of their mightiest exertions, and the supreme opportunity for their greatest exploits, must coincide with the apocalyptic upheaval marking the lowest ebb in mankind's fast-declining fortunes.' "

(PP 191)

It was in his most grave letter of 1954 to the American Bahá'í's that —
"Shoghi Effendi expatiated on this subject of a future conflict, its causes, its course, its outcome and its effect on America, in more detail and in more forceful language than he had ever before used..."

(PP 191)

"Alarmed we should be, but not paralysed...in August 1957, his secretary wrote on his behalf: 'He does not want the friends to be fearful, or to dwell upon the unpleasant possibilities of the future. They must have the attitude that, if they do their part, which is to accomplish the goals of the Ten Year Plan, they can be sure that God will do His part and watch over them.' 'As the situation in the world, and in your part of it, is steadily worsening, no time can be lost by the friends in rising to higher levels of devotion and service, and particularly of spiritual awareness. It is our duty to redeem as many of our fellow-men as we possibly can, whose hearts are enlightened, before some great catastrophe overtakes them, in which they will either be hopelessly swallowed up or come out purified and strengthened, and ready to serve. The more believers there are to stand forth as beacons in the darkness whenever that time does come, the better; hence the supreme importance of the teaching work of this time.' "

(PP 193)

With each warning, however, the Guardian always reminded us of the sources of strength we could always turn to for the accomplishment of every arduous goal.

"However severe the challenge, however sombre the world outlook, however limited the material resources of a hard-pressed adolescent community, the untapped sources of celestial strength from which it can draw are measureless, in their potencies, and will unhesitatingly pour forth their energizing influences if the necessary daily effort be made and the required sacrifices be willingly accepted."

(PP 193)

In order to continue to read the signs of the times we have but to study the messages from the Universal House of Justice which indicate the condition of the world and give us a view of the course humanity is following in terms similar to those used by the Guardian. In October 1967 that institution wrote —

"As humanity enters the dark heart of the age of transition our course is clear — the achievement of the assigned goals and the proclamation of Bahá'u'lláh's healing Message."

(WG 120-121)

In its Ridván message of 1969,

> "The continued progress of the Cause of God stands in vivid contrast to the chronic unrest afflicting human society, a contrast which the events of the past year, both within and without the Faith, have only served to intensify."
>
> (MUHJ 20)

And in November of that same year —

> "In the worsening world situation, fraught with pain of war, violence and the sudden uprooting of long-established institutions, can be seen the fulfillment of the prophecies of Bahá'u'lláh and the often-repeated warnings of the Master and the beloved Guardian about the inevitable fate of a lamentably defective social system, an unenlightened leadership and a rebellious and unbelieving humanity. Governments and peoples of both the developed and the developing nations, and other human institutions, secular and religious, finding themselves helpless to reverse the trend of the catastrophic events of the day, stand bewildered and overpowered by the magnitude and complexity of the problems facing them. At this fateful hour in human history, many, unfortunately, seem content to stand aside and wring their hands in despair or join in the babel of shouting and protestation which loudly objects, but offers no solution to the woes and afflictions plaguing our age.
>
> "Nevertheless a greater and greater number of thoughtful and fair-minded men and women are recognizing in the clamor of contention, grief and destruction, now reaching such horrendous proportions, the evidences of Divine Chastisement, and

turning their faces towards God are becoming increasingly receptive to His Word. Doubtless the present circumstances, though tragic and awful in their immediate consequences, are serving to sharpen the focus on the indispensability of the Teachings of Bahá'u'lláh to the needs of the present age..."
(MUHJ 33-34)

In January 1971 in its message to the Monrovia Conference, the Supreme Body wrote —
"Many of the gravest ills now afflicting the human race appear in acute form on the African Continent. Racial, tribal and religious prejudice, disunity of nations, the scourge of political factionalism, poverty and lack of education are obvious examples."
(MUHJ 62)

And in the Ridván message of 1972 they wrote —
"The divergence between the ways of the world and of the Cause of God becomes ever wider. And yet the two must come together. The Bahá'í Community must demonstrate in ever increasing measure its ability to redeem the disorderliness, the lack of cohesion, the permissiveness, the godlessness of modern society..."
(MUHJ 90)

The Ridván message of 1973 ends with: —
"The progress of the Cause of God gathers increasing momentum and one may with confidence look forward to the day when this Community, in God's good time, shall have traversed the stages predicated for it by its Guardian, and shall have raised on this tormented planet the fair mansions of God's Own

Kingdom wherein humanity may find surcease from its self-induced confusion and chaos and ruin, and the hatreds and violence of this time shall be transmuted into an abiding sense of world brotherhood and peace. All this shall be accomplished within Covenant of the everlasting Father, the Covenant of Bahá'u'lláh."

(MUHJ 120)

What is important to remember is that much suffering will be required in order to prepare the hearts of people to desire universal peace. There are those amongst humanity who wish to remain locked in the antiquated beliefs and institutions which keep people and nations from coming together. Not until all those beliefs and institutions are shown to be seen as obviously "lamentably defective" will the majority of nations and peoples of the earth be motivated to take measures to establish peace. Something beyond our imaginations will have to occur to motivate everyone to want peace. After we want it, then the nations of the world will take steps to establish it. But no concerted effort to seriously pursue peace will be *universally* taken until the bulk of nations are sufficiently motivated. And it is the motivation towards peace that the tribulations of this century will produce.

It is very similar to the time of Noah who called the people to God. Most of the people rejected His teachings. He warned the people of that day that a great flood of tribulation would come and that if people wanted to survive they should turn to Him. When the flood of afflictions was let loose, only those who had accepted His guidance and went to the Ark were saved. The Ark represented the teachings of the Prophet of God. Those teachings help us to float on top of the floodwaters rather than drown under them.

The Ark landed on a mountain. This may symbolize evolving to a higher level of development than mankind had achieved prior to the coming of Noah. This could not have happened without a flood of tribulations.

So it is today. Without an ocean of difficulties, a heedless humanity would hardly become motivated to leave its older, immature notions of prejudice and nationalism for more mature notions of world unity and peace.

As to whether or not mankind chooses to deepen its own distress further during the final years of the twentieth century, or chooses to avert the most horrible degree of suffering is a choice which still has to be made.

In "The Promise of World Peace" the Universal House of Justice indicates that such a choice is possible.

> "Whether peace is to be reached only after unimaginable horrors precipitated by humanity's stubborn clinging to old patterns of behaviour, or is to be embraced now by an act of consultative will, is the choice before all who inhabit the earth. At this critical juncture when the intractable problems confronting nations have been fused into one common concern for the whole world, failure to stem the tide of conflict and disorder would be unconscionably irresponsible." (PWP, 1)

If, by an act of consultative will, humanity can create the conditions essential to avert a nuclear holocaust, then the severity of the disastrous consequences of the disintegrative processes can be mitigated. If, however, such a choice is not made, the process of disintegration will reach a climax which will deepen the sorrows and suffering of all peoples.

CHAPTER FOUR

The Lesser Peace

ESTABLISHED BY THE NATIONS OF THE EARTH

The next major breakthrough humanity must make during the twentieth century, as a result of having experienced "the carnage, agony, and havoc of this great world convulsion" will be the Lesser Peace. It is distinguished from the Most Great Peace in that it is the precursor, and will be like an embryo when compared to the fuller development the Most Great Peace will involve. The consummation of the World Commonwealth will,

> "...by its very nature, be a gradual process, and must, as Bahá'u'lláh Himself anticipated, lead at first to the establishment of that Lesser Peace which the nations of the earth, as yet unconscious of His Revelation and yet unwittingly enforcing the general principles which He has enunciated, will themselves establish. This momentous and historic step, involving the reconstruction of mankind, as the result of the universal recognition of its oneness and wholeness, will bring in its wake the spiritualization of the masses, consequent to the recognition of the character, and the acknowledgment of the claims, of the Faith of Bahá'u'lláh — the essential condition to that ultimate fusion of all races, creeds, classes, and nations which must signalize the emergence of His New World Order."

(PDC 123)

As we have seen in Chapter 3, the nations of the earth, although "unconscious of His Revelation and yet unwittingly enforcing the general principles He has enunciated" formed the League of Nations after World War I and the United Nations after World War II. The Guardian pointed out how President Woodrow Wilson of the United States "voiced sentiments so akin to the principles animating the Cause of Bahá'u'lláh, and of having more than any other world leader, contributed to the creation of the League of Nations" (CF 36) which he described as the "precursor of that World Tribunal, which...the peoples and nations of the earth must needs unitedly establish." (GPB 305) The formation of both these international organizations whose express purpose was to provide a forum for the settlement of international disputes indicates that indeed society as a whole was responding in some degree to the unifying forces which have been released by Bahá'u'lláh's Revelation.

"The world's equilibrium hath been upset through the vibrating influence of this most great, this new World Order. Mankind's ordered life hath been revolutionized through the agency of this unique, this wondrous System — the like of which mortal eyes have never witnessed."

(WOB 109)

Principles and Features of the Lesser Peace

Towards the latter part of 1867 Bahá'u'lláh wrote His Tablets to the kings, whose temporal authority touched the lives of the masses of humanity in the nineteenth century. In His Tablets He revealed those essential teachings and principles required for the establishment of the Most

Great Peace and offered those rulers the priceless opportunity to usher in the highest form of peace the world had yet seen. Their vision, however, was faulty. All of them neglected this privilege, and careless of their station and the responsibility attending it, closed the door on what could have been a way to safeguard the lives and treasures of countless people around the world from the ravages of the convulsions which they would, as a consequence of the decision made by those rulers, have to experience throughout the twentieth century.

But Bahá'u'lláh, out of compassion for the masses of humanity, wrote again to several of those kings and leaders,

"Now that ye have refused the Most Great Peace, hold yet fast unto this the Lesser Peace, that haply ye may in some degree better your own condition and that of your dependents."

Expatiating on this Lesser Peace, He thus addresses in that same Tablet the rulers of the earth: —

"Be reconciled among yourselves, that ye may need no more armaments save in a measure to safeguard your territories and dominions...Be united, O Kings of the earth, for thereby will be tempest of discord be stilled amongst you, and your peoples find rest, if ye be of them that comprehend. Should any one among you take up arms against another, rise ye all against him, for this is naught but manifest justice."

(WOB 162)

Steps Leading to the Lesser Peace

" 'The time must come,' He, foreshadowing the tentative efforts that are now being made, has written, 'when the imperative necessity for the holding of a vast, an all embracing assemblage of men will be universally realized. The rulers and kings of the earth must needs attend it, and, participating in its deliberations, must consider such ways and means as will lay the foundations of the world's Great Peace among men...Should any king take up arms against another, all should unitedly arise and prevent him' "

(WOB 192)

The concepts of arms reduction and collective security are further expanded by 'Abdu'l-Bahá. He nurtures us with these ideas —

"True civilization will unfurl its banner in the midmost heart of the world whenever a certain number of its distinguished and high-minded sovereigns...shall, for the good and happiness of all mankind, arise, with firm resolve and clear vision, to establish the Cause of Universal Peace. They must make this Cause of Peace the object of general consultation, and seek by every means in their power to establish a Union of the Nations of the world. They must conclude a binding treaty and establish a covenant, the provisions of which shall be sound, inviolable and definite. They must proclaim it to all the world and obtain for it the sanction of all the human race. This supreme and noble undertaking — the real source of the peace and well-being of all the world — should be regarded as sacred by all that dwell on earth. All the forces of humanity must be mobilized to ensure the stability and permanence of this Most Great Covenant. In this all-embracing Pact the limits and frontiers of each and every nation should be clearly fixed, the principles underlying the relations of governments towards one another definitely laid down, and all international agreements and obligations ascertained. In like manner, the size of armaments of every government should be strictly limited, for if the preparation for war and the military forces of any nation should be allowed to increase, they will arouse the suspicion of others. The fundamental principle underlying this solemn Pact should be so fixed that if any government later violate any one of its provisions, all the governments on earth should arise to reduce it to utter submission, nay the human race as whole should resolve, with every power at its disposal, to destroy that government. Should this greatest of all remedies be applied to the sick body of the world, it will assuredly recover from its ills and will remain eternally safe and secure.

"Observe that if such a happy situation be forthcoming, no government would need continually to pile up the weapons of war, nor feel itself obliged to produce even new military weapons with which to conquer the human race. A small force for the purposes of internal security, the correction of criminal and disorderly elements and the prevention of local disturbances, would be required — no more. In this way the entire population would, first of all, be relieved of the crushing burden of expenditure currently imposed for military purposes, and secondly, great numbers of people would cease to devote their time to the continual devising of new weapons of destruction — those testimonials of greed and blood-thirstiness, so inconsistent with the gift of life — and would instead bend their efforts to the production of whatever will foster human existence and peace and well-being, and would become the cause of universal development and prosperity. Then every nation on earth will reign in honor and every people will be cradled in tranquility and content."

(SDC 64-66)

So far, then, the Writings describe the Lesser Peace as being brought about by the nations of the earth themselves, and those same nations will draw up a solemn Pact which stipulates their relations to one another and will involve the deliberate reduction of armaments and the means for collective action against any aggressor to the point of destroying that aggressive government. This implies, of course, that the nations of the world have united politically to an extent never before achieved. The Lesser Peace has been referred to by the Universal House of Justice as "the political unification of the world. Mankind at that time can be likened to a body that is unified but without life." (WG 133-134) In other words, as this will be an early form of international unity, it will not have yet blossomed into a spiritually-motivated, global civilization "sustained by its universal recognition of one God and by its allegiance to one common Revelation..." (WOB 204) That is the distinctive characteristic of the Most Great Peace.

The Lesser Peace will probably be motivated, as were the establishment of the League of Nations and the United Nations, by recognition of the dire need to find a way to resolve international disputes and conflicts which might result into a nuclear holocaust. It will be motivated by a need to survive — a need to reduce the chances of warfare from erupting, each successive war more disastrous than the previous one. But this time, mankind, having learned from its past shortcomings will adopt measures with some teeth. Whatever form it takes, all nations will agree to some type of collective security, arms reduction, and a "solemn Pact," as forecasted by 'Abdu'l-Bahá. An assemblage of world leaders will be established where world problems will receive serious attention until secure decisions and measures are adopted to ensure non-aggression.

The First and the Fifth Candles of Unity

The aforementioned passage from **Secret of Divine Civilization** is referring to the first candle of unity mentioned in the Tablet of the Seven Candles, by 'Abdu'l-Bahá:

"The first candle is unity in the political realm, the early glimmerings of which can now be discerned. The second candle is unity of thought in world undertakings, the consummation of which will ere long be witnessed. The third candle is unity in freedom which will surely come to pass. The fourth candle is unity in religion which is the cornerstone of the foundation itself, and which, by the power of God, will be revealed in all its splendor. The fifth candle is the unity of nations — a unity which in this century will be securely established, causing all the peoples of the world to regard themselves as citizens of one common fatherland. The sixth candle is unity of races, making all that dwell on earth peoples and kindreds of one race. The seventh candle is unity of language, i.e., the choice of a universal tongue in which all peoples will be instructed and converse. Each and every one of these will inevitably come to pass, inasmuch as the power of the Kingdom of God will aid and assist in their realization."

(WOB 39)

In his talk on the Lesser Peace in December 1984, Mr. Nakhjavání said —

"Someone asked Shoghi Effendi, in 1945, about the order of the appearance of the candles, and that is a point I have already mentioned. The Guardian's reply, written on his behalf on 19 November 1945, was this —

The Seven Lights of Unity will not necesasarily appear in the order given.'

"A question was asked about the second candle, which is unity of thought. The reply, in that same letter, was,

'A product of the second may well be universal culture.'

"But a far more important question was asked, more important than these two that I read to you. It was asked in 1936. This person who asked it is sitting right here in this room — Marion Hofman. God bless her for having asked this question... She asked him about the first and fifth candles. You recall the first candle was 'unity in the political realm, the early glimmerings of which can now be discerned,' and the fifth was the 'unity of nations — a unity which in this century will be securely established, causing all the peoples of the world to regard themselves as citizens of one common fatherland.' So she wanted to know what was the difference between these two. This was a very good question, a question of such importance that I cannot really in my lame words express appreciation to Marion for having asked it and to the beloved Gardian for his illuminating reply —

'With reference to your question concerning 'Abdu'l-Bahá's reference to —

"unity in the political realm" [first candle]; this unity should be clearly distinguished from the "unity of nations" [fifth candle]. The first is a unity which politically independent and sovereign states *achieve among themselves; while the second is one which is brought about between* nations, *the difference between a state and a nation being that the former, as you know, is a political entity without necessarily being homogeneous in race, whereas the second implies national as well as political homogeneity.'*

"What was 'Abdu'l-Bahá talking about? He was talking about two stages, two distinct stages in this process of the political unification of the world. One is the unity of sovereign governments, the other is the unity of peoples. One is a 'Union' or a 'Confederation' in terms of American history, the other is a 'federation'."

"I believe — and I may be totally wrong — that we have not yet seen realized the full implications of the first candle as yet, i.e., unity in the political realm. Now, some 66 years after the formation of the League of Nations and nearly 40 years after the establishment of the United Nations Organization, I don't think we have really achieved it. Truly the title 'United Nations,' I believe, is a misnomer in terms of 'Abdu'l-Bahá's and Shoghi Effendi's definitions. Maybe it should be called 'a partial Union or Confederation of most of the Governments of the world'...The whole concept of the power of veto is foreign to the concept of the Lesser Peace as advocated in our writings."

Mr. Nakhjavání further elucidated —
"A close study of the Writings of 'Abdu'l-Bahá will

reveal that this goal — I'm talking about the confederation now [union], that is the stage before the Federation, prior to the Lesser Peace — this goal will be achieved in two stages. Now this is my conclusion. I will read the texts and then you can arrive at your own conclusions. Here is the very celebrated passage of 'Abdu'l-Bahá in the *Secret of Divine Civilization* –

'True civilization will unfurl its banner in the midmost heart of the world whenever a certain number of its distinguished and high-minded sovereigns...'
"He didn't say 'all,' this is where the two stages come in; [earlier he indicated it would involve the United States and Canada] —

'shall, for the good and happiness of all mankind, arise, with firm resolve and clear vision, to establish the Cause of Universal Peace. They must make the Cause of Peace the object of general consultation, and seek by every means in their power to establish a Union of the nations of the world.'
"See how the words agree, the concepts agree.

'They must conclude a binding treaty and establish a covenant, the provisions of which shall be sound and inviolable and definite. They must proclaim it to all the world.'
"because they are not all the world,

'and obtain for it the sanction of all the human race.'
"As you see, we have first a group of leaders who spontaneously, as 'Abdu'l-Bahá says, will be forced into establishing peace, they have no choice. As 'Abdu'l-Bahá clearly tells us, and Shoghi Effendi confirms, these leaders will be led by the United States. They will

lay the foundations of peace, and submit their conclusions to the rest of the world; and then when these are accepted, this is just the fulfillment of the first candle.

"As to the stage of the Federation of the Nations of the World — the light of the fifth candle — according to what I understand — it will be revealed to men's eyes also in two stages. The preliminary stage of this Lesser Peace is when the nations of the world — and I am quoting Shoghi Effendi — will be 'unconscious' of Bahá'u'lláh's Revelation yet they will 'unwittingly' enforce 'the general principles which He has enunciated." So they are unaware of Bahá'u'lláh's station, yet they will be unwittingly enforcing general Bahá'í principles. Now, he has explained this in greater detail in a letter to an individual —

'With reference to the question you have asked concerning the time and means through which the Lesser and Most Great Peace, referred to by Bahá'u'lláh, will be established, following the coming World War. Your view that the Lesser Peace will come about through the political efforts of the states and nations of the world, and independently of any direct Bahá'í plan or effort,'

"I repeat, 'independently of any direct Bahá'í plan or effort,'

'and that the Most Great Peace [will be] established through the instrumentality of the believers, and by the direct operation of the laws and principles revealed by Bahá'u'lláh and the functioning of the Universal House of Justice as the supreme organ of the Bahá'í Super State — your view on this subject is quite correct and in full accord with the pronounce-

ments of the Guardian...'

"Now, what form will this Order take? I am talking now about the Lesser Peace that the world will unconsciously establish; this we cannot forecast. It will certainly be outside the orbit of our Faith, and as 'Abdu'l-Bahá has said, and I have repeated this several times tonight, all nations will be 'forced' into it. It is this peace which we know will take place in this century. It will be by general agreement. All the governments, 'Abdu'l-Bahá says, will disarm; and then He adds: they will disarm 'simultaneously.'

"But the second stage of this Lesser Peace, in my humble opinion, will occur after the year 2000. It will be a peace which is also described in our Writings as the Lesser Peace, but it will be established under the impact of the teachings of Bahá'u'lláh, the direct impact of His teachings, but it is still not yet the Most Great Peace. Shoghi Effendi fully outlines the features of this second stage of the Lesser Peace in "The Goal of a New World Order," written in November 1931, in the well-known passage beginning with the words: 'Some form of a World Super-State...' Three years later, in a letter written on his behalf in 1934, he made it clear that the passage in question did not by any means refer to the Bahá'í Commonwealth of the future, which is the hallmark of the Most Great Peace and the Golden Age of Bahá'u'lláh. The passage referred to this stage, this second stage of the Lesser Peace, that Bahá'u'lláh could well have had in mind when he wrote —

- *'It is incumbent upon the ministers of the House of Justice to promote the Lesser Peace so that the people of the earth may be relieved from the burden of exorbitant expenditures. This matter is imperative and absolutely essential, inasmuch as hostilities and conflict lie at the root of affliction and calamity.'*

"Now, back to Shoghi Effendi's statement and this, his celebrated passage in his "The Goal of a New World Order" —

'Some form of a world Super-State must needs be evolved, in whose favor all the nations of the world will have willingly ceded every claim to make war, certain rights to impose taxation and all rights to maintain armaments, except for purposes of maintaining internal order within their respective dominions. Such a state will have to include within its orbit an International Executive adequate to enforce supreme and unchallengeable authority on every recalcitrant member of the commonwealth; a World Parliament whose members shall be elected by the people in their respective countries and whose election shall be confirmed by their respective governments; and a Supreme Tribunal whose judgment will have a binding effect even in such cases where the parties concerned did not voluntarily agree to submit their case to its consideration. A world community in which all economic barriers will have been permanently demolished and the interdependence of Capital and Labor definitely recognized; in which the clamor of religious fanaticism and strife will have been forever stilled...'

"(This is where the influence of the Faith will have had its impact,)

'in which the flame of racial animosity will have been finally extinguished; in which a single code of international law — the product of the considered

judgement of the world's federated representatives — shall have as its sanction the instant and coercive intervention of the combined forces of the federated units; and finally a world community in which the fury of a capricious and militant nationalism will have been transmuted into an abiding consciousness of world citizenship — such indeed, appears, in its broadest outline, the Order anticipated by Bahá'u'lláh, an Order that shall come to be regarded as the fairest fruit of a slowly maturing age.'

"This is the outline of the Lesser Peace in its second, its fuller stage.

(See Table Six)

"As to the outline of the institutions and features of the Most Great Peace, that is something else altogether, and you find that in the words of Shoghi Effendi in **The World Order of Bahá'u'lláh**, pages 203-204, in his letter, "The Unfoldment of World Civilization." It is a different picture from the one described in the passage which I just read from, "The Goal of a New World Order."

"Now, there are a few other hints found in our Writings about the achievements of the Lesser Peace in both stages, in addition to the features Shoghi Effendi has included in what he calls his broad outline. I have extracted them, and I will read them quickly —

1. The limits and boundaries of each and every nation will be clearly fixed.
2. The relations of governments towards one another will be definitely laid down
3. The size of the armaments of each nation will be determined.

4. All international agreements and obligations will be checked and reviewed.
5. Steps will be taken to ensure that resources spent on the destruction of the human race will be used for universal development and prosperity.
6. Every nation on earth, whether its government is a constitutional monarchy or republican, will reign in honor, and its peoples will be cradled in tranquility and content.

TABLE SIX

The Lesser Peace

FORM AND OBJECTIVES AS IT EVOLVES

1. reconstruct and demilitarize the world
2. nations cede claims to make war
3. nations cede certain rights to impose taxes
4. nations cede all rights to maintain arms, except for internal order
5. international executive branch
6. world parliament
7. supreme tribunal
8. economic barriers removed
9. interdependence of capital and labour
10. religious fanaticism stilled
11. racial animosity extinguished
12. single code of international law
13. forces combined from federated units
14. militant nationalism trasmuted into consciousness of world citizenship

(WOB, pp 40-3)

"What I read are thoughts extracted from *The Secret of Divine Civilization* and talks given by 'Abdu'l-Bahá and published in *Star of the West*.

"Now, it would be an interesting subject for discussion if at some future date a study were made of the seven stages through which the Faith of God is to pass, as outlined by the Guardian, and correlate these stages with the steps that will lead humanity from its present phase of chaos, confusion and imbalance to the stage of orderliness and equilibrium, and ultimately to the splendors of the Most Great Peace.

"There is not time here for me to quote the words of 'Abdu'l-Bahá addressed to, or making reference to, bankers, financiers, calling on them to desist from lending money to projects which promote unjust wars; to soldiers, calling on them to petition their superiors not to be sent to fight wars inspired by cruelty and injustice; to experts and men of good will from various countries, to convene to adopt an international language; to mothers, to stop permitting their husbands, their sons, their brothers to be killed on battlefields; and finally to the philosophers of the West, to the wise leaders and sages of humanity, to the governments of the world, and to the rank and file of humanity, to find ways and means to stop all wars. Addressing all peoples, He says —

'Now is the appointed time! Now is the opportune time! Arise ye, show ye an effort, put ye forth an extraordinary power and unfurl the Flag of Universal Peace and restrain the irresistible fury of this raging torrent which is wreaking havoc and ruin everywhere.' "

(Nakhjavání, 1984)

Once a condition of non-aggression is attained then mankind will become free from the deprivations of intermittent warfare and can begin to turn its sights to more constructive pursuits. Only then will humanity begin to traverse a new path which will enable us to evolve a more mature and developed form of peace. Then will we be free to proceed with examining the bounties of political, economic, racial, international, and religious unity because we will not be ensnared in the condition of perpetual war.

We have really spent most of our history with our hands tied up in one way or another with preparations for war, actual warfare, or cleaning up the aftermath of war. It is only because wars have occured at intervals in most parts of the globe, and not constantly, that various cultures and civilizations have had some time to flourish. And even then, some very wonderful results have occurred. Imagine how much more mankind could attain in one century if it were free from war.

As limited as it will be, compared to the Most Great Peace, the Lesser Peace must be regarded as a "momentous and historic step, involving the reconstruction of mankind, as the result of the universal recognition of its oneness and wholeness..." (PDC 123) Further on this theme, the Guardian writes, "It calls for no less than the reconstruction and the demilitarization of the whole civilized world..." (WOB 43) Such an accomplishment will occur relatively soon.

During the Twentieth Century

As mentioned earlier, we know the Lesser Peace will be established within the Formative Age, the Age of Transition. (CF 6) Further, we know that the Universal House of Justice refers to the Lesser Peace as the "political unification of the world." (WG 133) The Guardian quoted 'Abdu'l-Bahá in the ***Promised Day is Come,***

"Behold, ...how its light is now dawning upon the world's darkened horizon. The first candle is unity in the political realm, the early glimmerings of which can now be discerned. The second candle is unity of thought in world undertakings, the consummation of which will erelong be witnessed. The third candle is unity in freedom which will surely come to pass. The fourth candle is unity in religion which is the cornerstone of the foundation itself, and which, by the power of God, will be revealed in all its splendor. ***The fifth candle is the unity of nations – a unity which, in this century, will be securely established, causing all the peoples of the world to regard themselves as citizens of one common fatherland...***"

(PDC 121) [emphasis added]

This latter passage would lead us to assume that the Lesser Peace, the political unification of nations, will be established before or at the end of the twentieth century.

In addition to the above passage of the Master's, the Guardian said that the completion of the administrative edifices on the far-flung arc on Mount Carmel,

"...will synchronize with two no less significant developments — the establishment of the Lesser Peace and the evolution of Bahá'í national and local institutions — the one outside and the other within the Bahá'í world..."

(MBW 74)

The Baháʼíʼs of the world are presently occupied with making necessary funds available to complete the remaining edifices on Mount Carmel and will be thusly occupied for at least the next ten years (1987-1997).

CONTRIBUTING FACTORS TO THE LESSER PEACE

Certain conditions must exist in order for the structure of the Lesser Peace to be established.

The Supreme Tribunal

> "The Supreme Tribunal is an aspect of a world superstate; the exact nature of its relationship to that state we cannot at present foresee...it will be a contributing factor in establishing the Lesser Peace."
>
> (LG 236)

From this it seems to be implied that a Supreme Tribunal is necessary, in some form, prior to the birth of the Lesser Peace, or during its early development in the Twenty first Century From ʻAbduʼl-Bahá we learn,

> "For example, the question of Universal Peace, about which Baháʼuʼlláh says that the Supreme Tribunal must be established; although the League of Nations has been brought into existence, yet it is incapable of establishing Universal Peace. But the Supreme Tribunal which Baháʼuʼlláh has described will fulfill this sacred task with the utmost might and power."
>
> (SWA 306)

It is interesting to explore at this point how the Supreme Tribunal will be formed.

"And His plan is this: that the national assemblies of each country and nation — that is to say parliaments — should elect two or three persons who are the choicest men of that nation who are well informed concerning international laws and relations between governments and aware of the essential needs of the world of humanity in this day. The number of these representatives should be in proportion to the number of inhabitants of that country. The election of these souls who are chosen by the national assembly, that is, the parliament, must be confirmed by the upper house, the congress and the cabinet and also by the president or monarch so these persons may be the elected ones of all the nation and the government. From among these people the members of the Supreme Tribunal will be elected, and all mankind will thus have a share therein, for every one of these delegates is fully representative of this nation."

(SWA 306)

If we look at this passage carefully it seems that the Supreme Tribunal, which is to contribute to the establishment of the Lesser Peace, will be one component of the "Union of the nations of the world" referred to earlier in this chapter and cited in the *Secret of Divine Civilization,* page 64.

These institutions should not be confused with Bahá'í institutions or the ultimate Bahá'í World Commonwealth of the future. The Union of nations and the Supreme Tribunal will be part of a world government which will be created by the nations of the world. This world government "...will herald the advent and lead to the final establishment of the World Order of Bahá'u'lláh." Referring to the International Executive, another institution of the

non-Bahá'í world government, the Guardian wrote,
> "The formation of this International Executive, which corresponds to the executive head or board in present-day national governments is but a step leading to the Bahá'í World Government of the future, and hence should not be identified with either the institution of the Guardianship or that of the International House of Justice."
> (LG 237)

Up to this time, the United Nations, like the League of Nations, has also not been capable of establishing Universal Peace. Therefore, we might conclude that prior to the end of this century the United Nations will either evolve into the Union of Nations from which the Supreme Tribunal will be elected, having a new level of authority and power vested in it by all its member nations, or it will be replaced by a new entity which will be that Union of Nations.

That it will not be institutions within the Faith that will usher in the Lesser Peace is reiterated when we examine the Constitution of the Universal House of Justice. That divine institution has the responsibility
> "To advance the interests of the Faith of God; to proclaim, propagate and teach its Message; to expand and consolidate the institutions of the Administrative Order; to usher in the World Order of Bahá'u'lláh;...to do its utmost for the realization of greater cordiality and amity amongst the nations and for the attainment of universal peace;..."
> (BW, Vol XV, 556)

The nations of the earth will usher in the Lesser Peace. The Universal House of Justice will usher in the Most

Great Peace associated with the World Order of Bahá'u'lláh.

It appears that although the "nations of the earth...will themselves" establish the Lesser Peace, the Universal House of Justice will do its part to encourage those same nations to make every effort in that direction. In this regard the House of Justice will promote the Lesser Peace, but will not actually be responsible for its establishment.

> "It is incumbent upon the ministers of the House of Justice to promote the Lesser Peace so that the people of the earth may be relieved from the burden of exorbitant expenditures. This matter is imperative and absolutely essential, inasmuch as hostilities and conflict lie at the root of affliction and calamity."
>
> (TB 89)

America Prepared for Preponderating Role

The second condition or contributing factor to the establishment of the Lesser Peace is that the American nation will have to take a role of leadership

> "in hoisting the standard of the Lesser Peace, in the unification of mankind, and in the establishment of world federal government on this planet."
>
> (CF, 127)

Some background on this subject may be helpful at this point. It was the Master, 'Abdu'l-Bahá, who made pronouncements regarding America and her destiny

> "...in the course of His epoch-making travels in 1912 in the North American continent..." "May this American Democracy be the first nation to establish the foundation of international agreement. May it be the

first nation to proclaim the unity of mankind. May it be the first to unfurl the standard of the Most Great Peace."

And again,

"The American people are indeed worthy of being the first to build the Tabernacle of the Great Peace, and proclaim the oneness of mankind... For America hath developed powers and capacities greater and more wonderful than other nations... The American nation is equipped and empowered to accomplish that which will adorn the pages of history, to become the envy of the world and be blest in both the East and the West for the triumph of its peoples... The American continent gives signs and evidences of very great advancement. Its future is even more promising, for its influence and illumination are far-reaching. It will lead all nations spiritually."

(ADJ 72)

In 1938 Shoghi Effendi wrote —

"A word, if the destiny of the American people, in its entirety, is to be correctly apprehended, should now be said regarding the orientation of that nation as a whole, and the trend of the affairs of its people. For no matter how ignorant of the Source from which those directing energies proceed, and however slow and laborious the process, it is becoming increasingly evident that the nation as a whole, whether through the agency of its government or otherwise, is gravitating, under the influence of forces that it can neither comprehend nor control, towards such associations and policies, wherein, as indicated by 'Abdu'l-Bahá, her true destiny must lie..."

(ADJ 73)

The Guardian then traced the path America must take prior to her involvement in World War II.

"A closer association with these Rupublics [of America], on the one hand, and an increased participation, in varying degrees, on the other, in the affairs of the whole world, as a result of recurrent international crises, appear as the most likely developments which the future has in store for that country. Delays must inevitably arise, setbacks must be suffered, in the course of that country's evolution towards its ultimate destiny. Nothing, however, can alter eventually that course ordained for it by the unerring pen of 'Abdu'l-Bahá. Its federal unity having already been achieved and its international institutions consolidated — a stage that marked its coming of age as a political entity — its further evolution, as a member of the family of nations, must, under circumstances that cannot at present be visualized, steadily continue. Such an evolution must persist until such time when that nation will, through the active and decisive part it will have played and the peaceful settlement of the affairs of mankind, have attained the plentitude of its powers and functions as an outstanding member, and component part, of a federated world...

"The world shaking ordeal which Bahá'u'lláh... has so graphically prophesied, may find it swept, to an unpredictable degree, into its vortex. Out of it will probably emerge, unlike its reactions to the last world conflict, consciously determined to seize its opportunity, to bring the full weight of its influence to bear upon the gigantic problems that such an ordeal must leave in its wake, and to exorcise forever, in conjunction with its sister nations of both the East and the West, the greatest curse which, from time immemorial, has afflicted and degraded the human race.

"Then and only then will the American nation, molded and purified in the crucible of a common war, inured to its rigors, and disciplined by its lessons, be in a position to raise its voice in the councils of the nations, itself lay the cornerstone of an enduring peace, proclaim the solidarity, the unity, and maturity of mankind, and assist in the settlement of the promised reign of righteousness on earth..."

(ADJ 75-76)

In June 1947, the Guardian wrote of the significant role America played in World War II, that it

"...redressed the balance, saved mankind the horrors and devastation and bloodshed involved in the prolongation of hostilities and decisively contributed...to the overthrow of the exponents of ideologies fundamentally at variance with the universal tenets of our faith."

(CF 36)

...and after the war she took "splendid initiative" to giving birth to the United Nations. Her full status however, of playing "a preponderating role...in the hoisting of the standard of the Lesser Peace" (CF 126) had not yet been attained. He goes on to say that the

"...road leading to its destiny is long, thorny and tortuous...Tribulations on a scale unprecedented in its history and calculated to purge its institutions, to purify the hearts of its people, to fuse its constituent elements, and to weld it into one entity with its sister nations in both hemispheres, are inevitable."

(CF 37)

It was not until 5 June 1954 that the beloved Guardian painted a picture of tribulations which the American nation as a whole would still have to experience before she would be fit to play her "preponderating role..." in the hoisting of the standard of the Lesser Peace. There were still major shortcomings which prevented America from fulfilling her role as a world spiritual leader. It was a result of the "steady and alarming deterioration in the standard of morality," and "cancerous materialism," the "chief factor in precipitating the dire ordeals and world-shaking crisis that must necessarily involve the burning of cities and the spread of terror and consternation in the hearts of men."

(CF 124-125)

The steadily worsening political situation between the two

> "...protagonists of two antagonistic schools of thought," ...the "multiplication, the diversity and the increasing destructive power of armaments to which both sides, in this world contest, caught in a whirlpool of fear, suspicion and hatred, and are rapidly contributing..." to "...the deterioration of a situation which, if not remedied, is bound to involve the American nation in a catastrophe of undreamed-of dimensions and of untold consequences to the social structure, the standard and the conception of the American people and government."

(CF 125-126)

In addition to these factors, a fourth factor — racial prejudice — would place an additional strain on the fabric of American society which,

> "...if allowed to drift, will, in the words of 'Abdu'l-Bahá, cause the streets of American cities to run with

blood, aggravating thereby the havoc which the fearful weapons of destruction, raining from the air, and amassed by a ruthless, a vigilant, a powerful and inveterate enemy, will wreak upon those same cities... The American nation...stands, indeed, from whichever angle one observes its immediate fortunes, in grave peril. The woes and tribulations which threaten it are partly avoidable, but mostly inevitable and God sent, for by reason of them a government and a people clinging tenaciously to the obsolescent doctrine of absolute sovereignty and upholding a political system, manifestly at variance with the needs of a world already contracted into a neighborhood and crying out for unity, will find itself purged of its anachronistic conceptions, and prepared to play a preponderating role, as foretold by 'Abdu'l-Bahá in the hoisting of the standard of the Lesser Peace, in the unification of mankind, and in the establishment of a world federal government on this planet. These same fiery tribulations will not only firmly weld the American nation to its sister nations in both hemispheres, but will through their cleansing effect, purge it thoroughly of the accumulated dross which the ingrained racial prejudice, rampant materialism, widespread ungodliness and moral laxity have combined, in the course of successive generations, to produce, and which have prevented her thus far from assuming the role of world spiritual leadership forecast by 'Abdu'l-Bahá's unerring pen — a role she is bound to fulfill through travail and sorrow.

(CF 125-127)

In summary, then, the second condition which must be present for the establishment of the Lesser Peace is that America must pass through "fiery tribulations" "on a scale unprecedented in its history" in order to be included with its sister nations in both hemispheres."

(CF 37)

The Retributive Calamity

The third factor which will pave the way for the establishment of the Lesser Peace will be the pervasive malaise which will have been the product of calamitous events afflicting the whole world.

It is interesting to note as we study the letters of the Guardian that he was still referring to this idea of a "calamity" until the last year of his life. In a letter to the Bahá'í's of the world, dated April 1957, he listed the —

"...signs and portents that must either herald of accompany the retributive calamity which, as decreed by Him Who is the Judge and Redeemer of mankind, must, sooner or later, afflict a society which, for the most part, and for over a century, has turned a deaf ear to the Voice of God's Messenger in this day — a calamity which must purge the human race of the dross of its age-long corruptions, and weld its component parts into a firmly-knit world-embracing fellowship — a fellowship destined, in the fullness of time, to be incorporated in the framework, and to be galvanized by the spiritualizing influences, of a mysteriously expanding, divinely appointed Order, and to flower, in the course of future Dispensations, into a Civilization, the like of which mankind has, at no stage in its evolution, witnessed."

(MBW 103)

"The signs and portents that must either herald or accompany the retributive calamity" are:

"The violent derangement of the world's equilibrium; the trembling that will seize the limbs of mankind; the radical transformation of human society; the rolling up of the present-day Order; the fundamental changes affecting the structure of government; the weakening of the pillars of religion; the rise of dictatorships; the spread of tyranny; the fall of monarchies; the decline of ecclesiastical institutions; the increase of anarchy and chaos; the extension and consolidation of the Movement of the Left; the fanning into flame of the smouldering fire of racial strife; the development of infernal engines of war; the burning of cities; and the contamination of the atmosphere of the earth."

(MBW 103)

Obviously, such a calamity, with the above heralding or accompanying events, will have to provide the environment in which the establishment of the Supreme Tribunal and the assumption of America as a leader in hoisting the standard of the Lesser Peace will take place.

The Nature of the Calamity

"We have no indication of exactly what nature the apocalyptic upheaval will be: it might be another war...but as students of our Bahá'í Writings it is clear that the longer the 'Divine Physician' (i.e. Bahá'u'lláh) is withheld from healing the ills of the world, the more severe will be the crises, and the more terrible the sufferings of the patient."

(LG 89)

It is not clear, then, in what form the calamity may come. It may be a more severe dose of what mankind foretasted in World Wars I and II or it might be something else, but however or in whatever form it comes, it is destined to make us all receptive to and ready for the establishment of world peace.

From the recent message on peace from the Universal House of Justice, we are reminded of the ultimate outcome.

> "A candid acknowledgment that prejudice, war and exploitation have been the expression of immature stages in a vast historical process and that the human race is today experiencing the unavoidable turmoil which marks its collective coming of age is not a reason for despair but a prerequisite to undertaking the stupendous enterprise of building a peaceful world. That such an enterprise is possible, that the necessary constructive forces do exist, that unifying social structures can be erected, is the theme we urge you to examine.
>
> Whatever suffering and turmoil the years immediately ahead may hold, however dark the immediate circumstances, the Bahá'í Community believes that humanity can confront this supreme trial with confidence in its ultimate outcome. Far from signaling the end of civilization, the conclusive changes towards which humanity is being evermore rigidly impelled will serve to release the potentialities inherent in the station of man and reveal 'the full measure of his destiny on earth, the innate excellence of his reality.'"

(PWP, 1985)

CHAPTER FIVE

Calamities: Prelude to The Lesser Peace

DISUNITY A DANGER

"Disunity is a danger that the nations and peoples of the earth can no longer endure; the consequences are too terrible to contemplate, too obvious to require any demonstration. 'The well-being of mankind,' Bahá'u'lláh wrote more than a century ago, 'its peace and security, are unattainable unless and until its unity is firmly established.' In observing that 'mankind is groaning, is dying to be led to unity, and to terminate its age-long martyrdom,' Shoghi Effendi further commented that: 'Unification of the whole of mankind is the hall-mark of the stage which human society is now approaching...' "

(PWP 11)

The Necessity of Upheavals

"Dear friends! The powerful operations of this titanic upheaval are comprehensible to none except such as have recognized the claims of both Bahá'u'lláh and the Báb. Their followers know full well whence it comes, and what it will ultimately lead to. Though ignorant of how far it will reach, they clearly recognize its genesis, are aware of its direction, acknowledge its necessity, observe confidently its mysterious processes, ardently pray for the mitigation of its severity, intelligently labor to assuage its fury, and anticipate, with undimmed vision, the consummation of the fears and hopes it must necessarily engender."

(PDC 4-5)

Retribution

"This judgment of God...is a retributory calamity and an act of holy and supreme discipline. It is at once a visitation from God and a cleansing process for all mankind. Its fires punish the perversity of the human race, and weld its component parts into one organic, indivisible, world-embracing community. Mankind, in these fateful years...is, as ordained by Him Who is both the Judge and the Redeemer of the human race, being simultaneously called upon to give account of its past actions, and is being purged and prepared for its future mission. It can neither escape the responsibilities of the past, nor shirk those of the future. God, the Vigilant, the Just, the Loving, the All-wise Ordainer, can...neither allow the sins of an unregenerate humanity, whether of omission or of commission, to go unpunished, nor will He be willing to abandon His children to their fate, and refuse them that culminating and blissful stage in their long, slow and painful evolution throughout the ages, which is at once their inalienable right and their true destiny."

(PDC 4-5)

Sins of Omission and Commission

One of the reasons humanity must be punished and purged is due to its complete negligence of the Message brought to it by Bahá'u'lláh, and the cruel persecution inflicted upon Him.

Calamities : Prelude to The Lesser Peace

"After a revolution of well nigh one hundred years what is it that the eye encounters as one surveys the international scene and looks back upon the early beginning of Bahá'í history? A world convulsed by the agonies of contending systems, races and nations, entangled in the mesh of its accumulated falsities, receding farther and farther from Him who is the sole Author of its destinies, and sinking deeper and deeper into a suicidal carnage which its neglect and persecution of Him Who is its Redeemer have precipitated."

(PDC 16)

Bahá'u'lláh has described in His own words the reception humanity accorded Him —

"All this generation...could offer us were wounds from its darts, and the only cup it proffered to Our lips was the cup of its venom. On Our neck We still bear the scar of chains, and upon Our body are imprinted the evidences of unyielding cruelty."

(PDC 13)

"O ye people of the world! Know, verily, that an unforeseen calamity followeth you, and grievous retribution awaiteth you. Think not that which ye have committed hath been effaced from My sight."..."We have a fixed time for you, O peoples. If ye fail, at the appointed hour, to turn towards God, He verily, will lay violent hold on you, and will cause grievous afflictions to assail you from every direction. How severe, indeed, is the chastisement with which your Lord will then chastise you!"

(WOB 201)

Chastisement for Human Perversity

In addition to our apathetic and/or cruel response to the Messenger of God for this age, we must also understand that we must be chastened for

"...the perversity of the human race in general, in casting itself adrift from those elementary principles which must, at all times, govern, and can alone safeguard, the life and progress of mankind. Humanity has, alas, with increasing insistence, preferred, instead of acknowledging and adoring the Spirit of God as embodied in His religion in this day, to worship those false idols, untruths and half truths, which are obscuring its religions, corrupting its spiritual life, convulsing its political institutions, corroding its social fabric, and shattering its economic structure. "Not only have the peoples of the earth ignored, and some of them even assailed, a faith which is at once the essence, the promise, the reconciler, and the unifier of all religions, but they have drifted away from their own religions, and set up on their subverted altars other gods wholly alien not only to the spirit but to the traditional forms of their ancient faiths."

(PDC 112)

"The chief idols in the desecrated temple of mankind are none other than the triple gods of Nationalism, Racialism and Communism, at whose alters governments and peoples, whether democratic or totalitarian, at peace or at war, of the East or of the West, Christian or Islamic, are, in various forms and in different degrees, now worshiping...The theories and policies, so unsound, so pernicious which deify the state and exalt the nation above mankind, which seek to subordinate the sister races of the world to one single race, which discriminate between the black and the white, and which tolerate the dominance of one privileged class over all others — these are the dark, the false, and crooked doctrines for which any man or people who believes in them, or acts upon them, must, sooner or later, incur the wrath and chastisement of God."

(PDC 113-114)

The Lamentably Defective Present Order

The third basic reason for this period of travail and suffering is to remove all antiquated notions and institutions which are obstacles in the path leading towards the unification of nations. "Soon will the present Order be rolled up, and a new one spread out in its stead." (WOB 161) "The signs of impending convulsions and chaos can now be discerned, inasmuch as the prevailing Order appeareth to be lamentably defective." (WOB 162)

"Must humanity, tormented as she now is, be afflicted with still severer tribulations ere their purifying influence can prepare her to enter the heavenly Kingdom destined to be established upon earth? Must the inauguration of so vast, so unique, so illumined an era in human history be ushered in by so great a catastrophe in human affairs as to recall, nay surpass, the appalling collapse of Roman civilization in the first centuries of the Christian Era? Must a series of profound convulsions stir and rock the human race ere Bahá'u'lláh can be enthroned in the hearts and consciences of the masses, ere His undisputed ascendancy is universally recognized, and the noble edifice of His World Order is reared and established?"

(WOB 201-202)

OUT OF HIS LOVE...

"God, however...does not only punish the wrongdoings of His children. He chastises because He is just, and He chastens because He loves. Having chastened them, He cannot, in His great mercy, leave them to their fate. Indeed, by the very act of chastening them He prepares them for the mission for which He has created them. 'My calamity is My providence,' He, by the Mouth of Bahá'u'lláh, has assured them, 'outwardly it is fire and vengeance, but inwardly it is light and mercy.'

"The flames which His Divine justice have kindled cleanse an unregenerate humanity, and fuse its discordant, its warring elements as no other agency can cleanse or fuse them. It is not only a retributory and destructive fire, but a disciplinary and creative process, whose aim is the salvation, through unification, of the entire planet. Mysteriously, slowly, and resistlessly God accomplishes His design, though the sight that meets our eyes in this day be the spectacle of a world hopelessly entangled in its own meshes, utterly careless of the Voice which, for a century, has been calling it to God, and miserably subservient to the siren voices which are attempting to lure it into the vast abyss."

(PDC 115-116)

It is as if the scale of justice is now being balanced. Due to mankind's excesses, the scale has gotten terribly out of balance through our racial prejudices, our materialism, and our attachment to national sovereignty. All those beliefs and attitudes which have weighted humanity toward the side of rebellious and irresponsible adolescence are now being violently torn away. The balance is coming to a more moderate position at which point our adolescence gives way to maturity, old prejudices are discarded for new, world-embracing concepts suited for an international global system.

Rites of Passage

In most cultures of the world the passage from youth to adulthood is usually marked by some special rite, event, or ceremony. In some cultures, a severe ordeal or test must be experienced by the young adult to prove he/she is ready to face the responsibilities of adulthood. Whether this test be to kill one's first animal in a hunt, or to collect a feather directly from the tail of a living eagle, or to be circumcised without anesthesia and without cries of pain, or to withstand severe beatings as a sign of endurance — the time of testing must be faced in order to be accepted by the community as an adult person. Such tests usually involve withstanding pain.

This is the social/cultural counterpart of the spiritual testing mankind as a whole is now undergoing —

"The ages of its infancy and childhood are past, never again to return, while the Great Age, the consummation of all ages, which must signalize the coming of age of the entire human race, is yet to come. The convulsions of this transitional and most turbulent period in the annals of humanity are the essential prerequisites, and herald the inevitable approach, of that Age of Ages, 'the time of the end,' in which the folly and tumult of strife that has, since the dawn of history, blackened the annals of mankind, will have been finally transmuted into the wisdom and the tranquility of an undisturbed, a universal, and lasting peace, in which the discord and separation of the children of men will have given way to the world wide reconciliation, and the complete unification of the diverse elements that constitute human society."

(PDC 117)

A Fitting Climax

"This will indeed be the fitting climax of that process of integration which, starting with the family, the smallest unit in the scale of human organization, must, after having called successively into being the tribe, the city-state, and the nation, continue to operate until it culminates in the unification of the world, the final object and the crowning glory of human evolution on this planet. It is this stage which humanity, willingly or unwillingly, is resistlessly approaching. It is for this stage that this vast, this fiery ordeal which humanity is experiencing is mysteriously paving the way."

(PDC 118)

CHAPTER SIX

Developing Constructive Responses : To Calamities

PROBABLE REACTIONS

Even though the Guardian spent much of his life explaining the nature of the turmoil humanity must experience during the Formative Age, even though we Bahá'ís have so much helpful information about the course which the world is following, and even though we may understand its necessity and work for the time when the fruits of this age will be visible, we still may, at times, become frightened about all of this. It is quite normal.

Imagine, then, how bewildered and hopeless the non-Bahá'í world must feel not having the same knowledge as we do on this subject. It must be very frightening for them. And the beloved Guardian describes some of the typical reactions displayed by people from all walks of life, around the world. Just to list a few reactions and conditions, we find in his letters these terms: sad, bewildered, vision dimmed, dismayed, paralyzed, sorrow, fears, disillusionment, perplexed, indignant, revolt, restless, shattered, despair, pain, contempt of discipline, rebellious, distress, disillusioned, misery, shame, distracted, etc.

These reactions are the consequence of not knowing why all these upheavals are occurring, not knowing what constructive purpose they are serving, and not knowing what to do in their midst. The Bahá'ís, however, have access, in the sacred Writings of the Faith, to concepts which explain and clarify the world situation, and what is more important, for mental, emotional, and spiritual survival, help us to find a constructive pathway to pursue amidst the chaos and debris of a tottering civilization.

SUSTAINING CONCEPTS

The Transforming Power of the Cause of God

The first concept that can heal our souls during periods of personal or global tribulations is this: that there is a power in the Cause of God which, if drawn upon, can transform ordinary people into quite extraordinary beings. Our characters can be transformed if we tap into this transforming power.

"These same people, though wrapt in all the veils of limitation, and despite the restraint of such observances, as soon as they drank the immortal draught of faith, from the cup of certitude, at the hand of the Manifestation of the All-Glorious, were so transformed that they would renounce for His sake their kindred, their substance, their lives, their beliefs, yea, all else save God! So overpowering was their yearning for God, so uplifting their transports of ecstatic delight, that the world and all that is therein faded before their eyes into nothingness. Have not this people exemplified the mysteries of "rebirth" and "return"? Hath it not been witnessed that these same people, ere they were endued with the new and wondrous grace of God, sought through innumerable devices, to ensure the protection of their lives against destruction? Would not a thorn fill them with terror, and the sight of a fox put them to flight? But once having been honoured with God's supreme distinction, and having been vouchsafed His bountiful grace, they would, if they were able, have freely offered up ten thousand lives in His path! Nay, their blessed souls, contemptuous of the cage of their bodies, would yearn for deliverance. A single warrior of that host would face and fight a multitude! And yet, how could they, but for the transformation wrought in their lives, be capable of manifesting such deeds which are contrary to the ways of men and incompatible with their worldly desires? "It is evident that nothing short of this mystic transformation could cause such spirit and behavior, so utterly unlike their previous habits and manners, to be made manifest in the world of being. For their agitation was turned into peace, their doubt into certitude, their timidity into courage. Such is the potency of the Divine Elixir, which, swift as the twinkling of an eye, transmuteth the souls of men!"

(KI 155-157)

And referring to the followers of the Báb and how this transforming power affected them, Bahá'u'lláh wrote:
"In every city, all the divines and dignitaries arose to hinder and repress them, and girded up the loins of malice, of envy, and tyranny for their suppression. How great the number of those holy souls, those essences of Justice, who, accused of tyranny, were put to death! And how many the embodiments of purity, who showed forth naught but true knowledge and stainless deeds, suffered an agonizing death! Notwithstanding all this, each of these holy beings, up to his last moment, breathed the Name of God, and soared in the realm of submission and resignation.

Such was the potency and transmuting influence which He exercised over them, that they ceased to cherish any desire but His will, and wedded their soul to His remembrance.

"...Instead of complaining, they rendered thanks unto God, and amidst the darkness of their anguish they revealed naught but radiant acquiescence to His will. ...The persecution and pain they inflicted on these holy and spiritual beings were regarded by them as means unto salvation, prosperity, and everlasting success. Hath the world, since the days of Adam, witnessed such tumult, such violent commotion? Notwithstanding all the torture they suffered, and manifold the afflictions they endured, they became the object of universal opprobrium and execration. Methinks patience was revealed only by virtue of their fortitude, and faithfulness itself was begotten only by their deeds."

(KI 234-236)

It is in man's nature to take whatever steps are possible, under normal conditions, to avoid pain to run from danger; basically to preserve himself from anything which threatens his survival.

"For self-love is kneaded into the very clay of man, and it is not possible that, without any hope of a substantial reward, he should neglect his own present material good...It is impossible for a human being to turn aside from his own selfish advantages and sacrifice his own good for the good of the community except through true religious faith."

(SDC 96-97)

Therefore, we know that in times when we are concerned with ourselves, whether it be our material or physical well-being, our jobs, our lives, our families, etc., it is possible to transcend our personal concerns and become aware of the larger concerns. Faith helps us to keep the broader picture in mind.

The End in the Beginning

Another sustaining concept is to be able to be clear-sighted enough to know what the ultimate goal is towards which tribulations are leading us. Without a clear picture of the fruits of suffering — the end, if you will — the suffering may seem absolutely useless and without purpose, and we lose our perspective and become swept up in the difficulties.

There is a beautiful story in The Seven Valleys of Bahá'u'lláh. It demonstrates this concept perfectly.

"There once was a lover who had sighed for long years in separation from his beloved, and wasted in the fire of remoteness. From the rule of love, his heart was empty of patience, and his body weary of his spirit; he reckoned life without her as a mockery, and time consumed him away. How many a day he found no rest in longing for her; how many a night the pain of her kept him from sleep; his body was worn to a sigh, his heart's wound had turned him to a cry of sorrow. He had given a thousand lives for one taste of the cup of her presence, but it availed him not. The doctors knew no cure for him and companions avoided his company; yea, physicians have no medicine for one sick of love, unless the favor of the beloved one deliver him.

"At last, the tree of his longing yielded the fruit of despair, and the fire of his hope fell to ashes. Then one night he could live no more, and he went out of his house, and made for the market place. All of a sudden, a watchman followed after him. He broke into a run, with the watchman following; then other watchmen came together, and barred every passage to the weary one. And the wretched one cried from his heart, and ran here and there, and moaned to himself: 'Surely this watchman is Izrá'íl my angel of death, following so fast upon me; or he is a tyrant of men, seeking to harm me!' His feet carried him on, the one bleeding with the arrow of love, and his heart lamented. Then he came to a garden wall, and with untold pain he scaled it, for it proved very high; and forgetting his life, he threw himself down to the garden.

"And there he beheld his beloved with a lamp in her hand, searching for a ring she had lost. When the heart-surrendered lover looked on his ravishing love, he drew a great breath and raised up his hands in prayer, crying: 'O God: Give thou glory to the watchman, and riches and long life. For the watchman was Gabriel, guiding this poor one; or he was Isráfil bringing life to this wretched one!'

"Indeed, his words were true, for he had found many a secret justice in this seeming tyranny of the watchman and seen how many a mercy lay hid behind the veil. Out of wrath, the guard had led him who was athirst in love's desert to the seat of his loved one, and lit up the dark night of absence with the light of reunion. He had driven one who was afar, into the garden of nearness, had guided an ailing soul to the heart's physician.

"Now if the lover could have looked ahead, he would have blessed the watchman at the start, and prayed on his behalf, and he would have seen that tyranny as justice; but since the end was veiled to him, he moaned and made his plaint in the beginning. Yet those who journey in the garden land of knowledge, because they see the end in the beginning, see peace in war and friendliness in anger."

(SV 13-15)

The above story is referring to the Valley of Knowledge in which the wayfarer

"...comes out of doubt into certitude...He in this station is content with the decree of God, and seeth war as peace, and findeth in death the secrets of everlasting life"..."The wayfarer in this Valley seeth in the fashionings of the True One nothing save clear providence."..."And if he meeteth with injustice he shall have patience, and if he cometh upon wrath he shall manifest love."

(SV 11-13)

One way to develop the ability, or the eye, for seeing the end in the beginning is to immerse ourselves in the sacred Writings explaining the nature, purpose and ultimate aim of the "titanic struggle" our world is experiencing in the Age of Transition. The end is graphically painted for us, as well as the intermediate steps leading to the end of the Formative Period. Without this perspective we would be as one blind and without perception.

STEPS FOR HANDLING THE STRESS OF WORLDWIDE AFFLICTIONS

Prayer: From Doubt into Certainty

How then can one pass from fear and anger to courage and resignation? There are at least four steps all of us can take to strengthen our feelings and perceptions during times of world-encompassing trails. The first step is: Prayer.

"The universal crisis affecting mankind is... essentially spiritual in its causes. The spirit of the age, taken on the whole, is irreligious. Man's outlook on life is too crude and materialistic to enable him to elevate himself into the higher realms of the spirit.

"It is this condition, so sadly morbid, into which society has fallen, that religion seeks to improve and transform. For the core of religious faith is that mystic feeling which unites man with God. This state of spiritual communion can be brought about and maintained by means of meditation and prayer. And this is the reason why Bahá'u'lláh has so much stressed the importance of worship. It is not sufficient for a believer merely to accept and observe the teachings. He should, in addition, cultivate the sense of spirituality which he can acquire chiefly by means of prayer. The Bahá'í Faith, like all other Divine Religions, is thus fundamentally mystic in character. Its chief goal is the development of the individual and society, through the acquisition of spiritual virtues and powers. It is the soul of man which has first to be fed. And this spiritual nourishment prayer can best provide. Laws and institutions, as viewed by Bahá'u'lláh, can become really effective only when our inner spiritual life has been perfected and transformed.

Otherwise religion will degenerate into a mere organization, and becomes a dead thing.
"The believers, particularly the young ones, should therefore fully realize the necessity of praying. For prayer is absolutely indispensable to their inner spiritual development, and this, as already stated, is the very foundation and purpose of the religion of God."

(DFE 33-34)

In our supplications, there are even specific prayers to ask God to help us change our weaknesses into strengths. For example, one of the morning prayers says"
"Thou art He Who changeth through His bidding abasement into glory, and weakness into strength, and powerlessness into might, and fear into calm, and doubt into certainty. No God is there but Thee, the Mighty, the Beneficent."

(BP 119)

The prayers for assistance, spiritual qualities, tests and difficulties, protection, families — so many prayers to help us find our way through the difficulties of life.
And when we feel like broken-winged birds, there is this sustaining and reassuring Tablet of Bahá'u'lláh,
"The Great Being saith: The Tongue of Wisdom proclaimeth: He that hath Me not is bereft of all things. Turn ye away from all that is on earth and seek none else but Me. I am the Sun of Wisdom and the Ocean of Knowledge. I cheer the faint and revive the dead. I am the guiding Light that illumineth the way. I am the royal Falcon on the arm of the Almighty. I unfold the drooping wings of every broken bird and start it on its flight."

(TB 169)

He must have anticipated what we would need to survive this Age, for He has surely spread a bountiful table of nourishing food to feed our souls for every Age, especially this Age of Transition.

'Abdu'l-Bahá, The Exemplar

The second thing we can do is to turn to the sacred Writings for examples of how the Central Figures of the Faith Themselves coped and survived great tribulations. For example, 'Abdu'l-Bahá shows us what attitutdes to adopt when our circumstances become oppressive —

"Rejoice in my bondage, O ye friends of God for it soweth the seeds of freedom; rejoice at my imprisonment, for it is the well-spring of salvation; be ye glad on account of my travail, for it leadeth to eternal ease...

"As for you, O ye lovers of God, make firm your steps in His Cause, with such resolve that ye shall not be shaken though the direst of calamities assail the world. By nothing, under no conditions, be ye perturbed. Be ye anchored fast as the mountains, be stars that dawn over the horizon of life, be bright lamps in the gatherings of unity, be souls humble and lowly in the presence of the friends, be innocent in heart. Be ye symbols of guidance and lights of godliness, severed from the world, clinging to the stronghold that is sure and strong, spreading abroad the spirit of life, riding the Ark of salvation..."

(SWA 241-242)

And again,

"O ye lovers of God! Do not dwell on what is coming to pass in this holy place, and be ye in no wise alarmed.

Whatsoever may happen is for the best, because affliction is but the essence of bounty, and sorrow and toil are mercy unalloyed, and anguish is peace of mind, and to make a sacrifice is to receive a gift, and whatsoever may come to pass hath issued from God's grace.

"See ye, therefore, to your own tasks: guide ye the people and educate them in the ways of 'Abdu'l-Bahá. Deliver to mankind this joyous message from the Abhá Realm. Rest not, by day or night; seek ye no moment's peace..."

(SWA 245)

Other sources show us how to keep ourselves "on track" while the society around us collapses and becomes increasingly derailed:

"The champion builders of Bahá'u'lláh's rising World Order must scale nobler heights of heroism as humanity plunges into greater depths of despair, degradation, dissension and distress. Let them forge ahead into the future serenely confident that the hour of their mightiest exertions and the supreme opportunity for their greatest exploits must coincide with the apocalyptic upheaval marking the lowest ebb in mankind's fast-declining fortunes."

(CF 58)

Serve the Cause and Teach

The third thing we can do is to take decisive, constructive action. Especially in times of great distress it is comforting to have a constructive course of action to follow. Rather than standing by idle, the Bahá'ís have a clear path of action before them. Service attracts confirmations.

"Alarmed we should be, but not paralyzed. In one of his last letters to a European National Spiritual Assembly in August 1957, his secretary wrote on his behalf: 'He does not want the friends to be fearful, or to dwell upon the unpleasant possibilities of the future. They must have the attitude that if they do their part, which is to accomplish the goals of the Ten Year Plan, they can be sure that God will do His part and watch over them.'

(PP 193)

Again,

" 'As the situation in the world, and in your part of it, is steadily worsening, no time can be lost by the friends in rising to higher levels of devotion and service, and particularly of spiritual awareness. It is our duty to redeem as many of our fellow-men as we possibly can, whose hearts are enlightened, before some catastrophe overtakes them, in which they will either be hopelessly swallowed up or come out purified and strengthened, and ready to serve. The more believers there are to stand forth as beacons in the darkness, whenever that time does come, the better; hence the supreme importance of the teaching work at this time.' "

(PP 193)

Our duty, in this Age, is —

"...however confused the scene, however dismal the present outlook, however circumscribed the resources we dispose of, to labor serenely, confidently, and unremittingly to lend our share of assistance, in whichever way circumstances may enable us, to the operation of the forces which, as marshalled and directed by Bahá'u'lláh, are leading humanity out of

the valley of misery and shame to the loftiest summits of power and glory."
(PDC 124)

"The opportunities which the turmoil of the present age presents, with all the sorrows which it evokes, the fears which it excites, the disillusionment which it produces, the perplexities which it creates, the indignation which it arouses, the revolt which it provokes, the grievances it engenders, the spirit of restless search which it awakens, must, in like manner, be exploited for the purpose of spreading far and wide the knowledge of the redemptive power of the faith of Bahá'u'lláh, and for enlisting fresh recruits in the ever-swelling army of His followers."
(ADJ 40)

And again, the Guardian reminds us how the Bahá'í community must view these ordeals as blessings in disguise which present us with opportunities which ordinary times lack, and it is these opportunities which we must seize, and the pitfalls which we must avoid.

"Who knows but that these few remaining, fast-fleeting years, may not be pregnant with events of unimaginable magnitude, with ordeals more severe than any humanity has yet experienced, with conflicts more devastating than any which have preceded them. Danger, however sinister, must, at no time, dim the radiance of their new-born faith. Strife and confusion, however bewildering, must never befog their vision. Tribulations, however afflictive, must never shatter their resolve. Denunciations, however clamorous, must never sap their loyalty. Upheavals, however cataclysmic, must never deflect their course.

The present Plan, embodying the budding hopes of a departed Master, must be pursued, relentlessly pursued, whatever may befall them in the future, however distracting the crises that may agitate their country or the world."

(ADJ 60)

Regardless of world conditions, the expansion of the Faith must proceed.

"There is no refuge in the world today except the Cause of Bahá'u'lláh. The believers must rest assured that, having the faith, they have everything. They must place their lives in the Hand of God, and, confident of His mercy and protection, go on teaching the Cause and serving it, no matter what happens."

(VP 21)

Single-Minded Devotion

And the fourth thing to do is to remain focused, single-minded, and have confidence that what is happening today will produce a wonderful outcome.

"Our task is to build the World Order of Bahá'u'lláh. Undeflected by the desperate expedients of those who seek to subdue the storm convulsing human life by political, economic, social, or educational programs, let us with single-minded devotion, and concentrating all our efforts on our objective, raise His Divine System, and sheltered within its impregnable stronghold, safe from the darts of doubtfulness, demonstrate a Bahá'í way of life..."

(WG 147)

"The working out of God's Major Plan proceeds mysteriously in ways directed by Him alone, but the

Minor Plan that He has given us to execute, as our part in His ground design for the redemption of mankind, is clearly delineated. It is to this work that we must devote all our energies, for there is no one else to do it..."

(WG 134)

"Far from yielding in their resolve, far from growing oblivious of their task, they should, at no time, however much affected by circumstances, forget that the synchronization of such world-shaking crises with the progressive unfoldment and fruition of their divinely appointed task is itself the work of Providence, the design of an inscrutable Wisdom, and the purpose of an all-compelling Will, a Will that directs and controls, in its own mysterious way, both the fortunes of the faith and the destinies of men.
"...Such simultaneous processes of rise and fall, of integration and of disintegration, of order and chaos, with their continuous and reciprocal reactions on each other, are but aspects of a greater Plan, one and indivisible, whose Source is God, whose Author is Bahá'u'lláh, the theatre of whose operations is the entire planet, and whose ultimate objectives are the unity of the human race and the peace of all mankind.
"Reflections such as these should steel the resolve of the entire Bahá'í community, should dissipate their forebodings, and arouse them to rededicate themselves to every single provision of that Divine Charter whose outline has been delineated for them by the pen of 'Abdu'l-Bahá!"

(ADJ 60)

And finally, pointing out our privileged position of being able to understand the meaning of the times we are living in, and the part we must play, the beloved Guardian wrote —

"Who else can be the blissful if not the community of the Most Great Name, whose world-embracing, continually consolidating activities constitute the one integrating process in a world whose institutions, secular as well as religious, are for the most part dissolving?...Of all the kindreds of the earth they alone can recognize, amidst the welter of a tempestuous age, the Hand of the Divine Redeemer that traces its course and controls its destinies. They alone are aware of the silent growth of that orderly world polity whose fabric they themselves are weaving.

"Conscious of their high calling, confident in the society-building power which their faith possesses, they press forward, undeterred and undismayed, in their efforts to fashion and perfect the necessary instruments wherein the embryonic World Order of Bahá'u'lláh can mature and develop. It is this building process, slow and unobtrusive, to which the life of the world-wide Bahá'í Community is wholly consecrated, that constitutes the one hope of a stricken society."

(WOB 194-195)

CHAPTER SEVEN

Opposition to the Faith of Bahá'u'lláh

Why Must There Be Opposition?

The forces operating in the Formative Age are forces opposing each other. On the one hand, the forces of integration, the building up of a new society through the teachings of Bahá'u'lláh, and on the other hand, the forces of disintegration which are violently sweeping away any idea or institution which is an obstacle to the unification of mankind.

Imagine, if you will, that you are someone who is dependent in some way on one of those dying institutions. Your income, your professional pursuits, or perhaps your social status might be tied to your position in one of these dying forms. You might not be pleased at all that your old support system is going under. You may, in your efforts to save your own position, try to keep the outmoded institution alive as long as possible. Or, you might abandon it, knowing it is futile, and attach yourself to a better institution. Or, worse, you may strike out in angry vengeance at any new institution which seems to be thriving in order to attempt to thwart its growth. We will probably see a variety of all these reactions as the world-encircling upheavals increase in their intensity.

"How can the beginnings of a world upheaval, unleashing forces that are so gravely deranging the social, the religious, the political, and the economic equilibrium of organized society, throwing into chaos and confusion political systems, social doctrines, social conceptions, cultural standards, religious associations, and trade relationships — how can such agitations, on a scale so vast, so unprecedented, fail to produce any repercussions on the institutions of a Faith of such tender age whose teachings have a direct and vital bearing on each of these spheres of human life and conduct?

"Little wonder, therefore, if they who are holding aloft the banner of so pervasive a Faith, so challenging a Cause, find themselves affected by the impact of these world-shaking forces. Little wonder if they find that in the midst of this whirlpool of contending passions their Freedom has been curtailed, their tenets condemned, their institutions assaulted, their motives maligned, their authority jeopardized, their claim rejected."

(ADJ 2)

That the Bahá'í Faith is a dynamic growing entity is becoming increasingly apparent, especially as the Faith has recently experienced such widespread attention by the highest councils of the world as a result of the repression of the Bahá'ís in Írán. Those who are jealous of its growth, especially as the traditional religious institutions collapse, will arise in increasing numbers to discredit this relatively new Faith.

"For let every earnest upholder of the Cause of Bahá'u'lláh realize that the storms which this struggling Faith of God must needs encounter, as the process of the disintegration of society advances, shall be fiercer than any which it has already experienced. Let him be aware that so soon as the full measure of the stupendous claim of the Faith of Bahá'u'lláh comes to be recognized by those time-honored and powerful strongholds of orthodoxy, whose deliberate aim is to maintain their stronghold over the thoughts and consciences of men, this infant Faith will have to contend with enemies more powerful and more insidious than the cruelest torture-mongers and the most fanatical clerics who have afflicted it in the past. What foes may not in the course of the convulsions that shall seize a dying civilization be brought into existence, who will reinforce the indignities which have already been heaped upon it!"

(WOB 17)

It seems from this passage that the deeper we penetrate into the Age of Transition, the more complete becomes the disintegration of the old order, and the more fierce become the enemies of the Faith. The motive is almost solely naked jealously.

"Fierce and manifold will be the assaults with which governments, races, classes and religions, jealous of its rising prestige and fearful of its consolidating strength, will seek to silence its voice and sap its foundations."

(MA 14)

"That the forces of irreligion, of a purely materialistic philosophy, of unconcealed paganism have been unloosed, are now spreading, and, by consolidating themselves, are beginning to invade some of the most powerful Christian institutions of the western world, no unbiased observer can fail to admit. That these institutions are becoming increasingly restive, that a few among them are already dimly aware of the pervasive influence of the Cause of Bahá'u'lláh, that they will, as their inherent strength deteriorates and their discipline relaxes, regard with deepening dismay the rise of His New World Order, and will gradually determine to assail it, that such an opposition will in turn accelerate their decline, few, if any, among those who are attentively watching the progress of His Faith would be inclined to question."

(WOB 180-181)

And by the following verse we can assume that the more the Faith becomes recognized and the more authority it exercises in the world, the more severe shall be the challenges which will be aimed at it.

"Peoples, nations, adherents of divers faiths, will jointly and successively arise to shatter its unity, to sap its force, and to degrade its holy name. They will assail not only the spirit which it inculcates, but the administration which is the channel, the instrument, the embodiment of that spirit. For as the authority with which Bahá'u'lláh has invested the future Bahá'í Commonwealth becomes more and more apparent, the fiercer shall be the challenge which from every quarter will be thrown at the verities it enshrines."

(WOB 18)

Who Will Attack the Faith?

" 'This day the powers of all the leaders of religion are directed towards the dispersion of the congregation of the All-Merciful, and the shattering of the Divine Edifice. The hosts of the world, whether material, cultural or political are from every side launching their assault, for the Cause is great, very great. Its greatness is, in this Day, clear and manifest to men's eyes' "

(ADJ 5)

" 'How great, how very great is the Cause! How very fierce the onslaught of all the peoples and kindreds of the earth. Ere long shall the clamor of the multitude throughout Africa, throughout America, the cry of the European and of the Turk, the groaning of India and China, be heard from far and near. One and all, they shall arise with all their power to resist His Cause,' "

(WOB 17)

The Guardian elucidates on the subject of who will challenge the Faith: "...organized forces of superstition, of corruption, and of unbelief...," and "...exponents of religious orthodoxy...and political leaders..." (CF 120). We will face "the fury of conservative forces, the opposition of vested interests, and the objections of a corrupt and pleasure-seeking generation..." and deal with "...the forces of fanaticism, of orthodoxy, of corruption, and of prejudice..."

(ADJ 35).

How Will the Cause be Opposed?

"...storms of abuse and ridicule, and campaigns of condemnation and misrepresentation, may be unloosed against them. Their Faith, they may soon find, has been assaulted, their motives misconstrued, their aims defamed, their aspirations divided, their institutions scorned, their influence belittled, their authority undermined, and their Cause, at times, deserted by a few who will either be incapable of appreciating the nature of their ideals, or unwilling to bear the brunt of the mounting criticisms which such a contest is sure to involve."

(ADJ 35)

"Peoples, nations, adherents of divers faiths will jointly and successively arise to shatter its unity, to sap its force, and to degrade its holy name. They will assail not only the spirit which it inculcates, but the administration which is the channel, the instrument, the embodiment of that spirit..."

(WOB 18)

Who Will Defend or Protect the Faith?

Within the Faith our first source of protection is the sacred Writings themselves which will offer guidance to both individuals and institutions during times of opposition.

"For nothing short of the explicit directions of their Book, and the surprisingly emphatic language with which they have clothed the provisions of their Will, could possibly safeguard the Faith for which they have both so gloriously labored all their lives. Nothing short of this could protect it from the heresies and calumnies with which denominations, peoples, and governments have endeavored, and will, with increasing vigor, endeavor to assail it in future."

(WOB 22)

Part of adhering to the sacred text, especially the Will and Testament of 'Abdu'l-Bahá, means to follow the guidance of all those institutions created in the Will, and before it, in the Writings of Bahá'u'lláh. All the divine institutions have the tasks of propagating the Faith and protecting it from division and disunity from within, and from attacks originating from without. That the beloved Guardian anticipated the institutions would play a major role in dealing with opposition to the Cause is evident in the following passages —

"The Administrative strongholds of a Faith, bound to be subjected on the one hand, to a severe spiritual challenge from within, through the inevitable impact of these devastating influences on its infant strength, and on the other, to the onslaught of ecclesiastical leaders, the traditional defenders of religious orthodoxy from without, must be multiplied and reinforced for the purposes of warding off the inevitable attacks of the assailants, and vindicating the ideals and the principles which animate their defenders, and of ensuring the ultimate victory and ascendancy of the faith itself over the nefarious elements seeking to undermine it from within, and its powerful detractors aiming at its extinction from without."

(CF 154)

We can all try to increase, through out teaching efforts, the number of Local Assemblies in our area, for they will play a big role in guiding the friends throughout the periods of opposition.

"The more strenuous the effort exerted daily and methodically, by the individual...to contribute...to the multiplication of Bahá'í isolated centers, groups and assemblies, and to raise...the number of its active and whole hearted supporters...the lighter will be the burden of the suspending contest that must be waged, sooner or later, ...between the rising institutions of Bahá'u'lláh's embryonic divinely appointed Order and the exponents of obsolescent doctrines and the defenders both secular and religious, of a corrupt and fast-declining society."

(CF 155)

And the Universal House of Justice alluded to the power which the institutions would wield during times of opposition when it wrote that we should

"...brace ourselves in preparation for the attacks that are bound to be directed against its victorious onward march...The time is ripe and the opportunities illimitable. We are not alone nor helpless. Sustained by our love for each other and given power through the Administrative Order — so laboriously erected by our beloved Guardian — the army of Light can achieve such victories as will astonish posterity."

(WG 120)

Hidden Springs of Celestial Strength

"That the Cause associated with the name of Bahá'u'lláh feeds itself upon those hidden springs of celestial strength which no force of human personality, whatever its glamour, can replace; that its reliance is solely upon that Mystic Source with which no worldly advantage, be it wealth, fame, or learning can compare; that it propagates itself by ways mysterious and utterly at variance with the standards accepted by the generality of mankind, will, if not already apparent, become increasingly manifest as it forges ahead towards fresh conquests in its struggle for the spiritual regeneration of mankind."

(WOB 51)

We have, in this chapter, looked primarily at the prophecies and predictions concerning opposition to the Faith, its results, and its necessity. We have also examined how the Faith will be attacked, who will attack it, and who will defend it. The latter dealt only with the role to be played by the institutions of the Faith.

The greatest struggle, however, will not be against the institutions. The greatest battle, as always, will be waged in the heart of every individual as he rises to conquer his lower self. It is this battlefield we will consider in our next chapter.

CHAPTER EIGHT

Cultivating Spiritual Responses to Opposition

THE FRUITS OF OPPOSITION – RE-FRAMING OUR PERSPECTIVE

Developing constructive, healthy and spiritual responses to a situation in which one or one's religion is being attacked, maligned, and misrepresented is similar to trying to respond warmly to a hail storm or blizzard. Although nature's storms are random and impersonal it is painful when one is the target for any kind of intentional abuse from other human beings. If all we can see is the abuse, then it will be very difficult indeed to respond in any other way than to "put them in their place!" One usually feels compelled to block the punch, or punch back. Or, one could try to avoid the whole scene by dropping out and disowning one's faith. Some have, in religious history, chosen for the latter course.

So, it requires that we re-frame this situation — put it in another context — one in which the deeper meaning and purpose can be seen. If we apply the same principle to this subject that we applied earlier to facing the calamities, we should try to see the "end in the beginning." For a clear vision of what fruits these attacks against the Bahá'í Faith will produce, we need but to turn to the Writings of the beloved Guardian —

"We should welcome, therefore, not only the open attacks which its avowed enemies persistently launch against it, but should also view as a blessing in disguise every storm of mischief with which they who apostatize their faith or claim to be its faithful exponents assail it from time to time. Instead of undermining the Faith, such assaults, both from within and from without, reinforce its foundations and excite the intensity of its flame. Designed to becloud its radiance, they proclaim to all the world the exalted character of its precepts, the completeness of its unity, the uniqueness of its position, and the pervasiveness of its influence."

(WOB 15-16)

"The tribulations attending the progressive unfoldment of the Faith of Bahá'u'lláh have indeed been such as to exceed in gravity those from which the religions of the past have suffered. Unlike those religions, however, these tribulations have failed utterly to impair its unity, or to create, even temporarily, a breach in the ranks of its adherents. It has not only survived these ordeals, but has emerged, purified and inviolate, endowed with greater capacity to face and surmount any crisis which its resistless march may engender in the future."

(GPB 410)

Just as suffering tends to purify individuals from their attachments to trivia and to turn them to basic spiritual issues, attacks against the Faith tend to purify it and its followers, and to strengthen them.

"The voice of criticism is a voice that indirectly reinforces the proclamation of its Cause. Unpopularity but serves to throw into greater relief the contrast between it and its adversaries; while ostracism is itself a magnetic power that must eventually win over to its camp the most vociferous and inveterate amongst its foes."

(ADJ 35)

The more negative attention the enemies of the Faith heap upon it, the more attention the Cause receives in general from a curious humanity, and those who were uninformed about its precepts, laws and institutions come to learn about them as a result of the voices of opposition.

"However, such denunciations — against you and the Bahá'í Faith can do no harm to the Cause at all; on the contrary they only serve to spread its name abroad and mark it as an independent religion."

(OMF 15)

The Rhythm of Growth

All living things go through various stages of growth and setbacks. So, too, with the Bahá'í Faith.

"The resistless march of the Faith of Bahá'u'lláh... propelled by the stimulating influences which the unwisdom of its enemies and the force latent within itself, both engender, resolves itself into a series of rhythmic pulsations, precipitated, on the one hand, through the explosive outbursts of its foes, and the vibrations of Divine Power, on the other, which speed it, with ever-increasing momentum, along that predestined course traced for it by the Hand of the Almighty."

(MA 15)

The time of crisis is followed by a time of triumph.

"Despite the blows levelled at its nascent strength, whether by the wielders of temporal and spiritual authority from without, or by the black-hearted foes from within, the Faith of Bahá'u'lláh had, far from breaking or bending, gone from strength to strength, from victory to victory. Indeed its history, if read aright, may be said to resolve itself into a series of pulsations, of alternating crisis and triumphs, leading it ever nearer to its divinely appointed destiny."

(GPB 409)

We can see, that just as spring follows winter, growth follows crisis, whether the crisis is faced by an individual or by an institution. If we walk through the door of crisis, opposition, or calamity we find a new place waiting for us. A place which is even more conducive to our personal growth because choosing to go through the door requires courage. And whenever courage is exercised we acquire a greater capacity to face the next difficulty with even more assurance and trust.

"Indeed this fresh ordeal that has, in pursuance of the mysterious dispensations of providence, afflicted the Faith, at this unexpected hour, far from dealing a fatal blow to its institutions or existence, should be regarded as a blessing in disguise, not a 'calamity' but a 'providence' of God, not a devastating flood but a 'gentle rain' on a 'green pasture,' a 'wick' and 'oil' unto the 'lamp' of His Faith; a 'nurture' for His Cause, 'water for that which has been planted in the hearts of men,' a 'Crown set on the head' of His Messenger for this day."

(CF 139)

Cultivating Spiritual Responses to Opposition

"After the Storm..."

"Ye beloved of God! When the winds blow severely, rains fall fiercely, the lightening flashes, the thunder roars, the bolt descends and storms of trial become severe, grieve not; for after the storm, verily, the divine spring will arrive, the hills and fields will become verdant, the expanses of grain will joyfully move, the earth will become covered with blossoms, the trees will be clothed with green garments and adorned with blossoms and fruits. Thus blessings become manifest in all countries. These favors are results of those storms and hurricanes..."

(TA, Vol 1, 12-14)

"Therefore, O ye beloved of God, be not grieved when people stand against you, persecute you, afflict and trouble you and say all manner of evil against you. The darkness will pass away and the light of the manifest signs will appear, the veil will be withdrawn and the Light of Reality will shine forth from the unseen (Kingdom) of El-Abhá. This we inform you before it occurs, so that when the hosts of people arise against you for my love, be not disturbed or troubled; nay rather, be firm as a mountain, for this persecution and reviling of the people upon you is a pre-ordained matter. Blessed is the soul who is firm in the path."

(TA, Vol 1, 12-14)

These Writings help us to reframe our thinking and direct us to see the end results even before they appear. This focus of the mind is invaluable during times of stress and crisis. Otherwise, we are left to dwell on the present ordeal and the pain, but our mind has nothing constructive to focus on, and the suffering, instead of leading to growth and wisdom, leads us to bitterness and confusion. So, our Writings guide us to develop a constructive and healthy attitude towards the process of opposition to the Bahá'ís and to the Bahá'í Faith. They also tell what to focus on: the fruits of tribulations.

As was said in previous chapters the world is, so to speak, unaware of its general condition of pregnancy. A midwife is needed to teach the world how to cope with its period of intense labor and how to prepare for the new infant, which in this century, will be the Lesser Peace. So, too, the analogy can be applied within the Bahá'í Community during its own unique periods of duress when it is undergoing opposition and persecution. In this case the midwife could be any Bahá'í who understands the fruits of persecution and who can transmit the sense of patient expectation, calm, assurance, and confidence that the bounties and blessings which are the results of this kind of suffering will be forthcoming.

Behavior Toward the Oppressors

In addition to a sound mental attitude, we are also given guidance as to what behavior is appropriate to demonstrate during periods of attack, misrepresentation and opposition.

> "You must make firm the feet at the time when these trials transpire, and demonstrate forbearance and patience. You must withstand them with the utmost love and kindness; consider their oppression and persecution as the caprice of children, and do not give any importance to whatever they do. For at the

end the illumination of the Kingdom will overwhelm the darkness of the world and the exaltation and grandeur of your station will become apparent and manifest..."

(OMF 7)

'Abdu'l-Bahá in Times of Persecution

Describing His response to vicious attacks, the Master wrote —

"O my spiritual loved ones! At a time when an ocean of trials and tribulations was surging up and flinging its waves to the heavens, when multitudes where assailing us and the tyrannical were inflicting upon us crushing wrongs — at such a time a band of individuals, intent on defaming us, allied themselves with our unkind brother, brought out a treatise that was filled with slanderous charges, and levelled accusations and calumnies against us.

"In this way they alarmed and confused the government authorities, and it is obvious what the condition of this captive then became, in this dilapidated fortress, and what terrible harm and mischief was done, far worse than words can tell. In spite of everything, this homeless prisoner remained inwardly tranquil and secure, trusting in the peerless Lord, yearning for whatever afflictions might have to be encountered in the pathway of God's love. For bolts of hate are, in our sight, but a gift of peace from Him, and mortal poison but a healing draught..."

(SWA 243)

"Act in such a way that your heart may be free from hatred. Let not your heart be offended with anyone. If someone commits an error and wrong toward you, you must instantly forgive him."

(DAL 118)

Bahá'u'lláh has clearly said in His Tablets that if you have an enemy, consider him not as an enemy. Do not simply be long-suffering; nay, rather love him. Your treatment of him should be that which is becoming to lovers. Do not even say that he is your enemy. Do not see any enemies. Though he be your murderer, see no enemy. Look upon him with the eye of friendship. Be mindful that you do not consider him as an enemy and simply tolerate him, for that is but stratagem and hypocrisy. This is not becoming of any soul. You must behold him as a friend. You must treat him well. This is right."

(SWA 267)

"In every instance let the friends be considerate and infinitely kind. Let them never be defeated by the malice of the people, by their aggression and their hate, no matter how intense. If others hurl their darts against you, offer them milk and honey in return; if they poison your lives, sweeten their souls; if they inflict a wound upon you, be a balm of their sores; if they sting you, hold to their lips a refreshing cup."

(SWA 24)

"O army of God! Beware lest ye harm any soul, or make any heart to sorrow; lest ye wound any man with your words, be he known to you or a stranger, be he friend or foe. Pray ye for all; ask ye that all be blessed, all be forgiven. Beware, beware, lest ye offend the feelings of another, even though he be an evil-doer, and he wish you ill. Look ye not upon the creatures, turn ye to their Creator. See ye not the never-yielding people, see but the Lord of Hosts. Gaze ye not down upon the dust, gaze upward at the shining sun, which hath caused every patch of darksome earth to glow with light.

"O army of God! When calamity striketh, be ye patient and composed. However afflictive your sufferings may be, stay ye undisturbed, and with perfect confidence in the abounding grace of God, brave ye the tempest of tribulations and fiery ordeals."

(SWA 73-74)

And let us share for a moment, some of the sufferings of 'Abdu'l-Bahá and observe how He responded to such tribulations at the hand of the enemies of the Cause:

"O ye my spiritual friends! For some time now the pressures have been severe, the restrictions as shackles of iron. This hopeless wronged one was left single and alone, for all the ways were barred. Friends were forbidden access to me, the trusted were shut away, the foe compassed me about, the evil watchers were fierce and bold. At every instant, fresh affliction. At every breath, new anguish. Both kin and stranger on the attack; indeed, one-time lovers, faithless and unpitying, were worse than foes as they rose up to harass me. None was there to defend. 'Abdu'l-Bahá, no helper, no protector, no ally, no champion. I was drowning in a shoreless sea, and ever beating upon my ears were the raven-croaking voices of the disloyal.

"At every daybreak, triple darkness. At eventide, stonehearted tyranny. And never a moment's peace, and never a balm for the spear's red wounds. From moment to moment, word would come of my exile to the Fezzan Sands; from hour to hour, I was to be cast into the endless sea. Now they would say that these homeless wanderers were ruined at last; again that the cross would soon be put to use. This wasted frame of mine was to be made the target for bullet or arrow; or again, this failing body was to be cut to ribbons by the sword. Our alien acquaintances could not contain themselves for joy, and our treacherous friends exalted. 'Praise be to God,' one would exclaim, 'Here is our dream come true.' And another, 'God be thanked, our spear-head found the heart.'

"Affliction beat upon this captive like the heavy rains of spring, and the victories of the malevolent swept down in a relentless flood, and still 'Abdu'l-Bahá remained happy and serene, and relied on the grace of the All-Merciful. That pain, that anguish was a paradise of all delights, those chains were the necklace of a king on a throne in heaven. Content with God's will, utterly resigned, my heart surrendered to whatever fate had in store, I was happy. For a boon companion, I had great joy.

"Finally a time came when the friends turned inconsolable, and abandoned all hope. It was then the morning dawned, and flooded all with unending light. The towering clouds were scattered, the dismal shadows fled. In that instant the fetters fell away, the chains were lifted from off the neck of this homeless one and hung round the neck of the foe. Those dire straits were changed to ease, and on the horizon of God's bounties the sun of hope rose up. All this was out of God's grace and his bestowals.

"And yet, from one point of view, this wanderer was saddened and despondent. For what pain, in the time to come, could I seek comfort? At the news of what granted wish could I rejoice? There was no more tyranny, no more affliction, no tragical events,

Cultivating Spiritual Responses to Opposition 147

no tribulations. My only joy in this swiftly-passing world was to tread the stony path of God and to endure hard tests and all material griefs. For otherwise these earthly life would prove barren and vain, and better would be death. The tree of being would produce no fruit; the sown field of this existence would yield no harvest. Thus it is my hope that once again some circumstance will make my cup of anguish to brim over, and that beauteous Love, that Slayer of souls, will dazzle the beholders again. Then will this heart be blissful, this soul be blessed."

The Master closes this excerpt with the following supplication —

"O Divine Providence! Lift to Thy lovers' lips a cup brimful of anguish. To the yearners on thy pathway, make sweetness but a sting, and poison honey-sweet. Set Thou our heads for ornaments on the points of spears. Make Thou our hearts the targets for pitiless arrows and darts. Raise Thou this withered soul to life on the martyr's field, make Thou this faded heart of drink the draught of tyranny, and thus grow fresh and fair once more. Make him to be drunk with the wine of Thine Eternal Covenant, make him a reveller holding high his cup. Help him to fling away his life; grant that for Thy sake, he be offered up. Thou art the Mighty, the Powerful. Thou art the Knower, the Seer, the Hearer."

(SWA 225-227)

It is so clear that the Master is re-framing, re-defining suffering for us. Rather than regarding tribulations as something to be avoided, He is educating us to welcome them. How opposite this is from the thinking of most people today. There are such rich rewards from undergoing calamities, especially in the path of God, that we do ourself a disservice if we should decide to flee from them.

This implies that tests and difficulties should be expected in this world, and especially while serving the Cause of God.

"The intent of what I wrote to thee in my previous letter was this, that when exalting the Word of God, there are trials to be met with, and calamities; and that in loving Him, at every moment there are hardships, torments, afflictions.

"It behoveth the individual first to value these ordeals, willingly accept them, and eagerly welcome them; only then should we proceed with teaching the Faith and exalting the Word of God.

"In such a state, no matter what may befall him in his love for God — harassment, reproach, vilification, curses, beatings, imprisonment, death — he will never be cast down, and his passion for the Divine Beauty will but gain in strength. This was what I meant.

"Otherwise, woe and misery to the soul that seeketh after comforts, riches, and earthly delights while neglecting to call God to mind! Because calamities encountered in God's pathway are, to 'Abdu'l-Bahá, but favour and grace, and in one of His Tablets that all-glorious Beauty hath declared: 'I never passed a tree but Mine heart addressed it saying: "O would that thou wert cut down in My name, and My body crucified upon thee!"' These were the words of the Most Great Name. This is His path. This is the way to His Realm of Might."

(SWA 240)

We have been focusing on developing a new mental attitude and behavioral responses towards tribulations. A deep study of the Bahá'í Writings is the first step in one's efforts to acquire such an attitude. 'Abdu'l-Bahá's example is yet another vehicle which can transport our thinking from the usual tendency to avoid tests to a new inclination to welcome them.

Bahá'ís in Írán – Living Testimonials

In recent years in Írán, and especially beginning in 1978, there have been countless praiseworthy examples of ordinary Bahá'ís who are applying these teachings in their everyday lives, in full view for our education and edification. To my mind, it is as if they are being recreated through the suffering they endure, and are becoming spiritual giants before our very eyes.

The following background information is taken from testimony about the continued persecution at the Bahá'í's in Írán given on May 22, 1984, before the U.S. House of Representatives, as it appears in the Congressional Record, pages H4280-4283-Ed.:

"Since the beginning of the Islamic revolution in Írán in 1979, more than 300 residences of Bahá'ís have been plundered or set on fire, and the people have nowhere to turn for help. One hundred and seventy Bahá'ís...have been killed by a variety of methods, but principally through execution by firing squads and by hangings.

In urban areas, properties belonging to hundreds of families have been seized, and in rural areas, orchards have been destroyed, farms and arable lands confiscated with no change for redress. The Ministry of Works and

Social Affairs of Írán formally instructed industrial and commercial institutions not to pay the salaries to Bahá'ís that were on their staff. More than 10,000 Bahá'ís employed in government offices or in the private sector have been summarily discharged, their rights to pensions and other employment benefits simply revoked, and in many cases demands were made of them to return the salaries they had earned. Students have been dismissed from universities and other institutions of higher learning, simply because they affirmed a belief in the Bahá'í religion. In most cities and provinces, Bahá'í children have been denied an education, the opportunity to attend school and to learn.

"Some 700 Bahá'ís including men, women and children are being held in various prisons today throughout Írán...In some prisons, Bahá'í prisoners are undergoing relentless torture in an effort on the part of authorities to force them to admit to false charges of engaging in espionage and acting against the Islamic Republic of Írán.

"For a period of months they have been subject to floggings of all parts of the body, particularly the legs and feet. Sometimes up to 400 strokes by wire. Cables have been administered to a single prisoner, and then that prisoner is forced to crawl back on his hands and knees to the darkness of his cell.

"Prisoners are regularly whipped in the head and face with thick plastic tubes in some prisons, and similar procedures are used, to a lesser degree, in others. A number of victims of torture have lost their sight and hearing; others, their mental competence.

"Religious shrines have been destroyed. The place of

the founding of the Bahá'í Faith was systematically torn down by the government..."

In 1983,

"...the Prosecutor General of Írán issued an edict banning all Bahá'í religious activities as criminal acts. Like the Nuremberg Laws, this edict establishes the so-called legal grounds for mass arrests and genocide...In response to this decree, elected leaders of the Bahá'í Faith in Írán did dissolve all Bahá'í institutions there, citing obedience, as they always do, to the civil law of the land. But, Mr. Speaker, this has done nothing to prevent more torture, more persecution, and more executions."

(WO 48-50)

I would like to share with you some of the true, documented accounts of the spiritual responses the Bahá'ís of Írán are demonstrating. The Hand of the Cause of God, Mr. Sears, in *A Cry from the Heart*, quotes from an open letter written in Yazd on November 3, 1981 —

"The Bahá'í men and women — particularly the women — are facing tribulations with such equanimity that no comparable example can be found even among the legendary heroines of the past. These women are in fact creating new legends through their patience, steadfastness, love and detachment. They have conquered the hearts of everyone and won the praises of all. The forces of hatred have been vanquished by the power of their Faith. When they are looted of their property, furniture and belongings, they part with them as they would with outworn dolls and play things, looking on as though they were spectators. They shower love upon those who come to take away their belongings as might an affectionate and indulgent parent who with a smile will give a worthless toy or plaything to a naughty child. It appears they even enjoy the naughtiness of these children.

"Such behavior has greatly influenced the hearts of the looters who are not great in number. Mr. K____, that heartless man who is the leader of those who are executing the Bahá'ís and confiscating their properties, and whose main task is to uproot the Faith in Yazd — is often seen entering the homes of the Bahá'ís who jest with him, saying, 'You have become one of us!' He even knows the nicknames of the Bahá'í children. If he does not make an appearance for some time the Bahá'ís tell him they miss him. Although Mr. K____ comes to take away their property or to send their loved ones to prison, they are pleasant to him, joke with him, inquire about his health. They even tell him that one day he should become a Bahá'í in order to understand the significance of what he is now doing.

"...The Bahá'ís of Yazd say that this unfeeling man, Mr. K____, is treated by them as a member of the family. When he comes to seize their furniture the young men of the family help him carry out the heavier pieces; when he arrives they invite him to join them at the table and give him sweets, fruits, even meals. After he has eaten he goes around the house and selects the furniture he wants to take away. If he does not have a vehicle available he gestures toward the selected articles of furniture and tells the owner, 'These are my trust with you, keep them safely until I return.' He sometimes even proposes that the family might buy back the furniture from him! The behavior of the long-suffering Bahá'ís in these appalling circumstances is unprecedented. They recognize that they are indeed giving away worthless dolls, as to an ignorant child."

(CFH 153-154)

Asadu'lláh Mu<u>kh</u>tárí was a Bahá'í who lived a simple life as a shepherd, with his family, in the town of Birjard. His body was found in the fields; he had been stoned to death. On several occasions his home had been looted and his herds stolen by ruffians in the town, because he was a Bahá'í.

On one occasion they tried to force him to recant his belief in Bahá'u'lláh and the Bahá'í Faith. He refused. They threatened to cut his throat. He remained calm and serene through it all.

"Fearlessly, he said to them: 'I have some excellent logs in my storage bin, and a container of kerosene.' He took a box of matches from his pocket and handed it to the ringleader. 'Here. Do as you please. I am at your mercy!

"The crowd hesitated at Asadu'lláh's bravery and contempt for their threats had shamed them. The old shepherd, firm as a rock, declared: 'Even if you burn me alive, I am still a Bahá'í. I will never give up my Faith.'

(CFH 138-139)

They threatened to return sometime. When they did, they found him alone in the fields, and stoned him to death.

"To regard one's enemies as one's well-wishers is indeed seen over and over again by the courageous believers in Írán. One believer, Mr. Mihdí Anvarí requested that his family distribute sweets among those who were to execute him, so that he might thank them for the privilege of dying for his religion.

(CFH 113)

The following extracts are from the accounts of the interrogations before executing ten Bahá'í women on June 18, 1983, in Shíráz. Such accounts display their complete steadfastness, bravery and the will to live and die for sacred principles.

Mrs. Túbá Zá'írpur had been in solitary confinement for 55 days and had become weak and ill. Another prisoner told of her imprisonment and trial —

"She had her first trial four days after she was imprisoned. For three consecutive days she was summoned for interrogation and was asked many questions; but the answers she gave did not satisfy the investigator. Each day they took her down to the basement and lashed her in order that she give the information they wanted...

"...On the first day she was lashed with fifty strokes, on the second day, on hundred strokes, and on the third day, seventy-four strokes, with cable whip, some on the soles of her feet and some on her back. The hundred strokes of the second day made her lose consciousness before they took her back to her cell in prison. The sore spots on her body were so painful that she could not sleep for many nights. Her toes were bleeding and toenails fell off as a result of injuries. In spite of all the suffering Mrs. Zá'írpur never complained. She prayed all the time. She was the embodiment of spiritual strength and resignation to the will of God, and a source of comfort to all of us.

She had dedicated her life to the service of the Cause of God and finally gave up her life and was honored with the crown of maryrdom in His path."

(WO 26-27)

And finally, the account of Moná Mahmúdnizhád, 16 years old, who, in her youth, was unafraid of the authorities who held her life in their hands. During the interrogation,

"...the religious magistrate, Mr. Qázáí, after insulting and humiliating her, said, 'Your father and mother have deceived and misled you.' In replay Moná said, 'Your honor, it is true that I learned about the Bahá'í Faith from my parents, but I have done my own reasoning. In the Bahá'í Faith one adheres to religion after investigation, not by imitation. You have read many of our books; you can read and find out for yourself. My father and mother did not insist on my accepting their belief; neither did they force me to become a Bahá'í. If the religious magistrate thinks I should abandon my belief, I will never do so, and prefer submitting to the order of execution'. The religious magistrate was astounded and said, 'Young girl, what do you know about religion?' Moná exclaimed, 'Your honour, I was brought here from the classroom in school; I have been in prison and going through trials for three months. What better proof of my religious certitude than my perseverance and steadfastness in the Faith? It is this Faith that gives me confidence to go through this trial in your presence...' The religious magistrate, impressed by Moná's sincerity, asked her to say a prayer. Moná put away the file and, with the usual respect and humbleness, recited a prayer by 'Abdu'l-Bahá... The religious magistrate remained silent for a while, then said to Moná, 'What harm did you find in Islám that you have turned to Bahá'ísm?' Moná's answer was, 'The foundation of all religions is one. From time to time, according to the exigencies of the time and place, God sends His Messenger to renew religion and guide the people in the right path. The Bahá'í religion upholds the truth in Islám, but if by Islám you mean the prevailing animosity, murder, and bloodshed in the country, a sample of which I have witnessed in prison, that is the reason I have chosen to be a Bahá'í.'"

(WO 28-29)

Of such substance are the present day Bahá'í heroes and heroines made. They prove, even to the doubter, the transforming power of the Cause. It changes ordinary men and women into mountains of strength in the face of oppression and tyranny; and into beings capable of loving their enemies and seeing them as well-wishers. It causes death to become an event to be embraced instead of shunned. It converts "...a gnat into an eagle, a drop into rivers and seas," and copper into gold.

Spiritual Endurance Releases Forces

"Every drop of blood shed by the valiant martyrs, every sigh heaved by the silent victims of oppression, every supplication for divine assistance offered by the faithful, has released, and will continue mysteriously to release, forces over which no antagonist of the Faith has any control, and which, as marshalled by the All-Watchful providence, has served to raise abroad the name and fame of the Faith to the masses of humanity, in all continents, millions of whom had previously been totally ignorant of the existence of the Faith or had but a superficial, and oft-times erroneous, understanding of its teachings and history.

"The current persecution has resulted in bringing the name and character of our beloved Faith to the attention of the world as never before in its history. As a direct result of the protests sent by the world-wide community of the Most Great Name to the rulers in Írán, of the representations made to the media when those protests were ignored, of direct approach by Bahá'í institutions at national and international levels, to governments, communities of nations, international agencies and the United Nations itself, the Faith of Bahá'u'lláh has not only been given sympathetic attention in the world's councils, but also its merits and violated rights have been discussed and resolutions of protest sent to the Iranian authorities by sovereign governments, singly and in unison. The world's leading newspapers, followed by the local press, have presented sympathetic accounts of the Faith to millions of readers, while television and radio stations are increasingly making the persecutions in Írán the subject of their programmes. Commercial publishing houses are beginning to commission books about the Faith.

"Indeed, this new move of persecution sweeping the cradle of the Faith may well be seen as a blessing in disguise, a 'providence' whose 'calamity' is, as always, borne heroically by the beloved Persian community. It may be regarded as the latest move in God's Major Plan, another trumpet blast to awaken the heedless from their slumber and a golden opportunity offered to the Bahá'ís to demonstrate once again their unity and fellowship before the eyes of a declining and skeptical world, to proclaim with full force the Message of Bahá'u'lláh to high and low alike, to establish the reverence of our Faith for Islám and its Prophet, to assert the principles of non-interference in political activities and obedience to government which stand at the very core of our Faith, and to provide comfort and solace to the breasts of the serene sufferers and steadfast heroes in the forefront of a persecuted community. Our motto in these days of world-gloom should be the Words of God addressed to the Blessed Beauty Himself! 'When the swords flash, go forward! When the shafts fly, press onward.!' "

(UHJ, January 26, 1982)

May We Be Worthy

"Dearly beloved friends, upon us devolves the supreme obligation to stand by His side, to fight His battles and to win His victory. May we prove ourselves worthy of His trust."

(BA 123)

"Shoghi Effendi perceived in the organic life of the Cause a dialectic of victory and crisis. The unprecedented triumphs, generated by the adamantine steadfastness of the Iranian friends, will inevitably provoke opposition to test and increase our strength. Let every Bahá'í in the world be assured that whatever may befall this growing Faith of God is but incontrovertible evidence of the loving care with which the King of Glory and His martyred Herald, through the incomparable Centre of His Covenant and our beloved Guardian, are preparing His humble followers for ultimate and magnificent triumph..."

(UHJ, January 2, 1986)

CHAPTER NINE

Women : The Missing Factor in Establishing Peace

CREATING THE CLIMATE FOR PEACE

"The emancipation of women, the achievement of full equality between the sexes, is one of the most important, though less acknowledged prerequisites of peace. The denial of such equality perpetuates an injustice against one half of the world's population and promotes in men harmful attitudes and habits that are carried from the family to the workplace, to political life, and ultimately to international relations. There are no grounds, moral, practical, or biological, upon which such denial can be justified. Only as women are welcomed into full partnership in all fields of human endeavor will the moral and psychological climate be created in which international peace can emerge."

(UHJ, Oct. 1985)

Let us explore how women will help create the proper "moral and psychological climate" for world peace.

First of all, we are in a new age — one which requires the development of a balance of human virtues and qualities. The world has tended to appreciate more forceful qualities in the past, perhaps because humanity was involved with basic physical survival. Now, humanity is on the verge of attaining maturity — a new period in which the focus on the physical developments of the past must give way to the higher developments of the mind and spirit. This new age will be one of refining our basic accomplishments, polishing and attending to the higher needs of our nature.

"The world in the past has been ruled by force and man has dominated over woman by reason of his more forceful and aggressive qualities of both body and mind. But the scales are already shifting; force is losing its weight, and mental alertness, intuition, and the spiritual qualities of love and service, in which woman is strong, are gaining ascendancy. Hence the new age will be an age less masculine and more permeated with the feminine ideals, or so to speak more exactly, will be an age in which masculine and feminine elements of civilization will be more properly balanced."

(SW, Vol. 9, No. 7, 87)

"The world of humanity has two wings — one is women and the other men. Not until both wings are equally developed can the bird fly. Should one wing remain weak, flight is impossible. Not until the world of women becomes equal to the world of men in the acquisition of virtues and perfections, can success and prosperity be attained as they ought to be."

(BWF 288)

We can assume from the above passage that the participation of women, one half of the globe's population, is so vital to achieving any human goal beyond superficial attainment, that the bird of humanity is simply not going to leave the ground without her full strength. A bird cannot fly with only one wing. Compared to the level of achievement humanity could reach when both sexes are equally developed, what we have attained thus far, has been, relatively speaking, quite limited.

Mothers and Peace

The special attributes which women have developed through the ages of bringing new life to the world and nurturing new life are essential qualities in the greater social equation.

'Abdu'l-Bahá emphasizes this in the following passage —
> "Thus, imbued with the same virtues as man, rising through all the degrees of human attainment, women will become the peers of men, and until this equality is established, true progress and attainment for the human race will not be facilitated...
>
> "The evident reasons underlying this are as follows: Woman by nature is opposed to war; she is an advocate of peace. Children are reared and brought up by the mothers who give them the first principles of education and labor assiduously in their behalf. Consider, for instance, a mother who has tenderly reared a son for twenty years to the age of maturity. Surely she will not consent to having that son torn asunder and killed in the field of battle. Therefore, as woman advances toward the degree of man in power and privilege, with the right of vote and control in human government, most assuredly war will cease; for woman is naturally the most devoted and staunch advocate of international peace."
>
> (PUP 375)

There is something very powerful about bearing the ordeals of motherhood. It tends to produce qualities in the mother, if she assumes the responsibilities associated with bringing a child into the world, which are essential for the preservation of humanity. Consider the following —

> "The most momentous question of this day is international peace and arbitration, and universal peace is impossible without universal suffrage. Children are educated by the women. The mother bears the troubles and anxieties of rearing the child, undergoes the ordeal of birth and training. Therefore, it is most difficult for mothers to send to the battlefield those upon whom they have lavished such love and care. Consider a son reared and trained for twenty years by a devoted mother. What sleepless nights and restless, anxious days she has spent! Having brought him through dangers and difficulties to the age of maturity, how agonizing then to sacrifice him upon the battlefield! Therefore, mothers will not sanction war nor be satisfied with it. So it will come to pass that when women participate fully and equally in the affairs of the world, when they enter confidently and capably the great arena of laws and politics, war will cease for woman will be the obstacle and hindrance to it. This is true and without doubt." (PUP 134-135)

It seems that when women, especially mothers, become fully involved in the decision-making, policy-making processes which affect international relations, they will help put priorities right by focusing on life-giving and life-sustaining measures rather than life-endangering measures.

In order to be qualified to participate in the affairs of the world, women must receive the same education as men.

Women : The Missing Factor in Establishing Peace

"...therefore, the principle of religion has been revealed by Bahá'u'lláh that woman must be given the privilege of equal education with man and full right to his prerogatives. That is to say, there must be no difference in the education of male and female in order that womankind may develop equal capacity and importance with man in the social and economic equation. Then the world will attain unity and harmony. In past ages humanity has been defective and inefficient because it has been incomplete. War and its ravages have blighted the world; the education of woman will be a mighty step toward its abolition and ending, for she will use her whole influence against war. Woman rears the child and educates the youth to maturity. She will refuse to give her sons for sacrifice upon the field of battle. In truth, she will be the greatest factor in establishing universal peace and international arbitration. Assuredly, woman will abolish warfare among mankind. Inasmuch as human society consists of two parts, the male and female, each the complement of the other, the happiness and stability of humanity cannot be assured unless both are perfected. Therefore, the standard and status of man and woman must become equalized."

(PUP 108)

In a sense, the missing link to peace is woman. It cannot be attained without her. She will make the final difference, and will tip the balance from war toward world peace. Therefore, it is to the continued detriment of all members of the human race to continue to place any obstacle in her way. If we do not open wide the doors to all women to get the best education and to enter all arenas of human endeavor, we are retarding the establishment of peace.

"Therefore, strive to show in the world that woman are most capable and efficient, that their hearts are more tender and susceptible than the hearts of men, that they are more philanthropic and responsive toward the needy and suffering, that they are inflexibly opposed to war and are lovers of peace. Strive that the ideal of international peace may become realized through the efforts of womankind for man is more inclined to war than woman, and a real evidence of woman's superiority will be her service and efficiency in the establishment of universal peace."

(PUP 284)

Education: First Priority to Women

The education of women to equip her for her roles as mother and peace-maker is so essential to the upliftment of the human race that the Bahá'í teachings are emphatic that she should be given the first priority to be educated.

"The cause of universal education, which has already enlisted in its service an army of dedicated people from every faith and nation, deserves, the utmost support that the governments of the world can lend it. For ignorance is indisputably the principal reason for the decline and fall of peoples and the perpetuation of prejudice. No nation can achieve success unless education is accorded all its citizens. Lack of resources limits the ability of many nations to fulfill this necessity, imposing a certain ordering of priorities. The decision-making agencies involved would do well to consider giving first priority to the education of women and girls, since it is through educated mothers that the benefits of knowledge can be most effectively and rapidly diffused throughout society. In keeping with the requirements of the times, consideration should also be given to teaching the concept of world citizenship as part of the standard education of every child."

(UHJ, October, 1985)

The Responsibility of Men to Encourage Women

It is interesting to note that the Bahá'í Writings encourage men to encourage women. 'Abdu'l-Bahá stated long ago —

"In brief, the assumption of superiority of man will continue to be depressing to the evolution of woman, as if her attainment to equality was creationally impossible; woman's aspiration toward advancement will be checked by it, and she will gradually become hopeless. On the contrary, we must declare that her capacity is equal, even greater than man's. This will inspire her with hope and ambition, and her susceptibilities for advancement will continually increase. She must not be told and taught that she is weaker and inferior in capacity and qualification. If a pupil is told that his intelligence is less than his fellow pupils, it is a very great drawback and handicap to his progress. He must be encouraged to advance by the statement, "You are most capable, and if you endeavor, you will attain the highest degree...and let it be known once more that until woman and man recognize and realize equality, social and political progress here or any where will not be possible."

(PUP 76-77)

In a momentous message from the Universal House of Justice dated October, 1985, entitled, "The Promise of Peace", we are reminded that: "Only as women are <u>welcomed</u> into full partnership in all fields of human endeavor will the moral and psychological climate be created in which international peace can emerge." The word "welcomed" is significant. Who is doing the welcoming? Those who are already involved in all arenas of endeavor, namely, men. And again, "The decision-making agencies involved would do well to consider giving first priority to the education of women and girls..." (UHJ, October, 1985) It is predominantly men who hold the vast majority of decision-making positions at the local, national, and international levels. So, theirs is the duty to invite, welcome and encourage the participation of women in order to redress the balance of power between the sexes.

The Responsibility of Women to Develop Themselves

The principle of equality between both sexes has often been espoused by radical people and movements, which has, unfortunately, led to an uncomfortable feeling about equal rights for women among many. Although the principle itself is true, just, and timely, the appropriate expression of this principle needs to be manifested. Some expressions are more effective and productive than others.

"Demonstrations of force such as are now taking place in England are neither becoming nor effective in the cause of womanhood and equality. Woman must especially devote her energies and abilities toward the industrial and agricultural sciences, seeking to assist mankind in that which is most needful. By this means she will demonstrate capability and insure recognition of equality in the social and economic equation."

(PUP 283)

Only by studying, acquiring knowledge and skills, in formal, or informal settings can women become equipped with those useful proficiencies needed in the world today.

"The realities of things have been revealed in this radiant century, and that which is true must come to the surface. Among the realities is the principle of the equality of man and woman — equal rights and prerogatives in all things appertaining to humanity. But while this principle of equality is true, it is likewise true that woman must prove her capacity and aptitude, must show forth evidences of equality. She must become proficient in the arts and sciences and prove by her accomplishments that her abilities and powers have merely been latent."

(PUP 283)

The Right to Vote

It is difficult to believe that today there are still some parts of the world where women do not have the right to vote. On the subject of women's suffrage 'Abdu'l-Bahá wrote:

"Another fact of equal importance in bringing about international peace is woman's suffrage. That is to say, when perfect equality shall be established between men and woman, peace may be realized for the simple reason that womankind in general will never favor warfare. Woman will not be willing to allow those whom they have so tenderly cared for to go to the battlefield. When they shall have a vote, they will oppose any cause of warfare..."

(PUP 167)

Not all women can become scientists, artists or professionals. Just as all men cannot be in policy-making positions, so all women will not be able to occupy those posts. But the masses of women, poor or rich, from the East or the West, can express their opinion through the means of the vote, one of this century's most basic forms of self-expression.

"In this Revelation of Bahá'u'lláh, the women go neck and neck with the men. In no movement will they be left behind. Their rights with men are equal in degree. They will enter all the administrative branches of politics. They will attain in all such a degree as will be considered the very highest station of the world of humanity and will take part in all affairs. Rest ye assured...For His Holiness Bahá'u'lláh Has Willed It So!...At the time of elections the right to vote is the inalienable right of women and the entrance of women into all human departments is an irrefutable and incontrovertible question. No soul can retard or prevent it."

(PT 182)

Although I have been unable to find any reference specifically pertaining to the role women will play in bringing about the Lesser Peace, it is clear that when a certain number of the nations of the world present the "Pact", mentioned in Chapter Four, to the rest of the world, and all the world must sanction it, women, in their capacity as fifty percent of the voting citizens of the world, will have a significant role in bringing the Lesser Peace into being.

Women : The Missing Factor in Establishing Peace

In addition, women, and particularly mothers, will have to find ways to assert their influence, through the vote, and through all legitimate channels open to them, to insist that their sons not be allowed to participate in war.

Women's Superior Capacities

"The woman is indeed of the greater importance to the race. She has the greater burden and the greater work. Look at the vegetable and animal worlds. The palm which carries the fruit is the tree most prized by the date grower. The Arab knows that for a long journey the mare has the longest wind. For greater strength and fierceness, the lioness is more dreaded by the hunter than the lion. The mere size of the brain has been proved to be no measure of superiority. The woman has greater moral courage than the man; she has also special gifts which enable her to govern in moments of danger and crisis. If necessary she can become a warrior...Taken in general, women today have a stronger sense of religion than men. The woman's intuition is more correct; she is more receptive and her intelligence is quicker. The day is coming when woman will claim her superiority to man."

(ABL 104-108)

"In some respects woman is superior to man. She is more tender-hearted, more receptive, her intuition is more intense."

(LG 500)

"Therefore, strive to show in the human world that women are most capable and efficient, that their hearts are more tender and susceptible than the hearts of men, that they are more philanthropic and responsive toward the needy and suffering, that they are inflexibly opposed to war and are lovers of peace."

(PUP, 284)

Women Arising for Peace

"What 'Abdu'l-Bahá meant about the women arising for peace is that it is a matter which vitally affects women, and when they form a conscious and overwhelming mass of public opinion against war there can be no war. The Bahá'í women are already organized through being members of the Faith and the administrative Order. No further organization is needed. But they should, through teaching and through active moral support they give to every movement directed towards peace, seek to exert a strong influence on other women's minds in regard to this essential matter."

(LG 497)

All departments of human endeavor, all branches of arts, sciences, trade, crafts and professions are open to both sexes, according to the Bahá'í teachings. Power, control and authority are to be shared between men and women; decisions and policies are to be made jointly by men and women. All rights and prerogatives which have already been granted to men are also to be granted to women.

CHAPTER TEN

Our Children and Youth in the Age of Frustration

Out of the deepest concern for humanity's welfare Bahá'u'lláh spent 40 long years of imprisonment, exile, and persecution in bequeathing to the world all the spiritual and social teachings we would need to pass from adolescence to maturity, and evolve the golden civilization destined by God for us to inherit.

After Him, 'Abdu'l-Bahá, toiled for almost 30 years as the sole Interpreter of Bahá'u'lláh's Revelation, to amplify and elucidate those sacred truths, and to call the world to peace.

After 'Abdu'l-Bahá, the beloved Guardian, Shoghi Effendi, penned countless letters and books for the Bahá'ís everywhere, outlining clearly the twin processes of integration and destruction which are leading humanity through the twentieth century to the Lesser Peace. He poured out his appeals to the believers to understand the operations of these processes in order that we could play our part in the unfolding drama of world unity with greater assurance, hope, and confidence. He spent 36 years guiding us through world upheavals, pointing out to us the ultimate goal, and holding our hands through world-engulfing tribulations. Always realistic in appraising world events, even at their darkest, reminding us of the light at the end of the tunnel.

And now, the unfailing promises from the Universal House of Justice, provide us with the same loving support and guidance as we approach the final "unavoidable tumult which marks its collective coming of age" and "confront this supreme trial with confidence in its ultimate outcome."

(UHJ, October, 1985)

All the Central Figures of the Faith, and especially the beloved Guardian, lovingly prepared us for the vast changes which we would experience during the twentieth century as a prelude to the Lesser Peace. Their Writings provide the full picture of the promise of peace, as well as the thorny road leading to that peace. Where would we be today without Their realistic appraisal of humanity's arduous journey? How would we fare if they had only told us of the promise and failed to educate us about the ordeals necessary to attain that promised goal? We would be caught unaware, and perhaps we would doubt that peace could ever be attained as we might become bogged down in the mire of difficulties. We might lose faith in God altogether, if we felt misled.

We have, however, been richly prepared for these times. It is as if we were being trained by a master to climb Mt. Everest. Months in advance of the climb, we are taken through exercises, climbing smaller mountains, learning how to endure various climates and to scale precipices, experiencing inordinately low temperatures, adjusting to thinness of air — all in preparation for the greatest climb of all. Without such preparation, the novice would have to leave the climb, never to behold the panoramic view awaiting those who attain the mountain peak.

THE PROMISE AND THE THREAT

All the religions of the past, and now, the Bahá'í Faith, have taught mankind of the Promise. The Promise is many things — the paradise of a faithful soul when reaching its Best Beloved, or the promise of eternal life after death, or the promise of peace on earth, etc. Religion also teaches us of the Threat — the dire consequences of ignoring the salutary teachings and commandments of God. Such a threat can be interpreted as meaning that one will suffer the torment of knowing one has displeased God, of being conscious of being deprived of His presence, or it may be assigned more earthbound meanings, such as war, which is always likened to Hell. It is this balanced view of life here and hereafter which Bahá'u'lláh encourages be taught to children —

> "Schools must first train the children in the principles of religion, so that the Promise and the Threat, recorded in the Books of God, may prevent them from the things forbidden and adorn them with the mantle of the commandments; but this in such a way that it may not injure the children by resulting in ignorant fanaticism and bigotry."
>
> (TB 68)

Just as Bahá'u'lláh had, so 'Abdu'l-Bahá and Shoghi Effendi painstakingly prepared us for the times in which we are living, so we as parents must help our children understand what is happening in the world around them. But, we must educate them in the same manner in which the Central Figures educated mankind — with love, assurance, and careful wisdom. The sacred Writings themselves provide us with the loving balance.

The Promise

The Revelation of Bahá'u'lláh emphasizes the promise of a world civilization, free from prejudice, and providing each individual with the opportunities and the means of fulfilling his or her divine nature. It promises every soul that struggles to follow God's guidance the rewards of spiritual virtues. It promises society and individuals a chance to attain maturity — when the fairest fruits of intellectual, physical, emotional, and spiritual development will appear on the tree of human endeavor.

The fact that Bahá'u'lláh's dispensation will last at least 1,000 years, and that His Cycle will endure 500,000 years demonstrates the positive emphasis on civilization building, rather than on destruction. It is a dispensation and cycle which primarily concerns itself with the evolution of the soul and society. These aspects are easy to convey to children of all ages, in a way that gives them hope and encouragement to grow up and assist in bringing these good things into being. As parents it is our obligation to stress these promises and be informed about their fulfillment.

The Threat

With all things organic, there is the second aspect — that of consequences. For every choice there is a consequence. Pleasant or unpleasant, all consequences can be viewed as educational in their nature. If we choose to touch a hot stove, the consequence is that our fingers will get burned and there will be pain. That can teach us to protect our hand by using a hot-pad before touching the stove next time. Consequences teach us lessons.

Bahá'u'lláh did not shy away from this reality —
> "O people of God! that which traineth the world is Justice, for it is upheld by two pillars, reward and punishment. These two pillars are the sources of life to the world."
>
> (TB 27)

To deny punishment for wrongdoing, or to deny the consequences to poor choices, is to deprive humanity of half its source of life. For both are necessary — reward or punishment. How else could we realize when we make mistakes? If there were no consequences to mistakes, there could be no learning of doing things in a better way.

If the kings and political rulers of the world make poor choices, e.g., they proceed in believing that their own ideas, religion, or country are superior to those of other leaders, the world will suffer the consequences. If they continue to resolve conflicts between themselves through force, instead of negotiation, arbitration, etc., we will continue to have wars, economic crises, oppression and tyranny.

These matters are so obvious to children. There are available in local lending libraries stories readily understood by children of all ages, which effectively illustrate the negative consequences of prejudice.

Since Bahá'u'lláh taught the necessity of tests, difficulties, and punishment, we as parents must also share these teachings with our children, and in such a way as to foster true understanding of their purpose. The following passages may help us explain the purpose of tests, difficulties, and punishments to our children, as they contain analogies which are easy for children to grasp.

"Know thou that ordeals are of two kinds: One kind is to test the soul, and the other is punishment for actions, that which is for testing educational and developmental and that which is the punishment of deeds is severe retribution.

"The father and the teacher sometimes humor the children and sometimes discipline them. This discipline is for educational purposes and is indeed to give them true happiness; it is absolute kindness and true providence. Although in appearance it is wrath, yet in reality it is kindness. Although outwardly it is an ordeal, yet inwardly it is purifying water.

"Verily, in both cases we must supplicate and implore and commune to the Divine threshold in order to be patient in ordeals.

"Tests are benefits from God, for which we should thank Him. Grief and sorrow do not come to us by chance, they are sent to us by the Divine mercy for our own perfection.

"While man is happy he may forget his God; but when grief comes and sorrows overwhelm him, then will he remember his Father Who is in Heaven, and Who is able to deliver him from his humiliations.

"Men who suffer not, attain no perfection. The plant most pruned by the gardeners is that one which, when the summer comes, will have the most beautiful blossoms and the most abundant fruit.

"The laborer cuts up the earth with his plough, and from that earth comes the rich and plentiful harvest. The more a man is chastened, the greater is the harvest of spiritual virtues shown forth by him. A soldier is no good general until he has been in the front of the fiercest battle and has received the deepest wounds."

(DAL 89-90)

"The mind and spirit of man advance when he is tried by suffering...Just as the plough furrows the earth deeply, purifying it of weeds and thistles, so suffering and tribulation free man from the petty affairs of this worldly life until he arrives at a state of complete detachment. His attitude in this world will be that of divine happiness."

(DAL 90)

"To the sincere ones, tests are as a gift from God, the Exalted, for a heroic person hasteneth with the utmost joy and gladness, to the tests of a violent battlefield, but the coward is afraid and trembles and utters moaning and lamentation. Likewise an expert student prepares and memorizes his lessions and exercises with the utmost effort, and in the day of examination he appears with infinite joy before the master. Likewise, the pure gold shines radiantly in the fire of test. Consequently, it is made clear that for holy souls, trials are as the gift of God, the Exalted; but for weak souls they are an unexpected calamity..."

(DAL 90)

We parents need to become well-versed in these aspects of Bahá'í teachings for they are so helpful in interpreting the meaning of ordeals, both on the personal level as well as on the global level. We must use wisdom in teaching our children the necessity of tests, rewards, and punishments, in our own personal lives, and explain the events in today's world to them in light of God's ultimate purpose for man. Each child's needs must be assessed in regard to this theme. Some children are susceptible to upsets and depression, others are more buoyant. These teachings should not be given so as to frighten children, but rather, in a timely fashion to assist them in understanding why life is especially difficult these days. However, we must not become morbid and dwell only on life's troubles. We must emphasize the fruits and results of troubles.

GROWING UP

It is hard to grow up — learning to walk brings bumps and bruises; tying shoes is very difficult at first; learning to share, solving arguments, passing tests at school — it's all hard. Now, humanity is going through one of the most difficult periods it must pass through, from adolescence to adulthood. That is why the world is going through such major changes. Such changes are essential, and are a part of the natural growing-up process.

We can use the stories from many of the world's cultures regarding the rites of passage to explain to our children that young adults must go through great difficulties and ordeals to be ready to face the responsibilities of adulthood. The world is about to go through great difficulties and ordeals to be ready to face the responsibilities of adulthood. The world is about to go through this rite of passage, too. The House of Justice refers to it as the "supreme trial."

(UHJ, October, 1985)

We must always approach these difficulties in light of the ***fruits they bear:*** personal growth and global peace.

WORDS AS MILD AS MILK

We will have to use our imaginations to gently teach our children the basically happy Bahá'í perspective about this world, and its last adolescent struggles. We must find the balance in our explanations — an overdose of anything is dangerous. And the balance can be found in the sacred Writings themselves.

"Every word is endowed with spirit, therefore the speaker or expounder should carefully deliver his words at the appropriate time and place, for the impression which each word maketh is clearly evident and perceptible. The Great Being saith: One word may be likened to fire, another unto light, and the influence which both exert is manifest in the world. Therefore, an enlightened man of wisdom should primarily speak with words as mild as milk, that the children of men may be nurtured and edified thereby and may attain the ultimate goal of human existence which is the station of true understanding and nobility. And likewise He saith: One word is like unto springtime causing the tender saplings of the rose garden of knowledge to become verdant and flourishing, while another word is even as a deadly poison. It behoveth a prudent man of wisdom to speak with utmost leniency and forbearance so that the sweetness of his words induce everyone to attain that which befitteth man's station."

(TB 172)

"O My Name! Utterance must needs possess penetrating power. For if bereft of this quality it would fail to exert influence. And this penetrating influence dependeth on the spirit being pure and the hearts stainless. Likewise, it needeth moderation, without which the hearer would be unable to bear it, rather he would manifest opposition from the very outset. And moderation will be obtained by blending utterance with the tokens of divine wisdom which are recorded in the sacred Books and Tablets. Thus when the essence of one's utterance is endowed with these two requisites it will prove highly effective and will be the prime factor in transforming the souls of men. This is the station of supreme victory and celestial dominion. Whoso attaineth thereto is invested with the power to teach the Cause of God and to prevail over the hearts and minds of men."

(TB 198-199)

Keeping the Perspective

We have primarily focused on the Bahá'í Writings which deal with the processes which will lead mankind to peace. Although this is a very large topic and could be studied in more depth and breadth, we must remember that the Revelation of Bahá'u'lláh covers a far more vast set of themes than this one. For His teachings are as the ocean, and this theme is only one of its many pearls to be garnered.

As we expand and deepen our own awareness of His teachings, we can share them all with our children, indeed, we must. This will ensure that they receive a balanced Bahá'í education.

Inheritors of the Lesser Peace

Our children today will be the inheritors of the Lesser Peace. Born in a period of transition, they will witness the final collapse of an outworn order, and will contribute, by serving the Faith, indirectly to the establishment of the Lesser Peace. They will serve directly in the evolution of Bahá'u'lláh World Order — a parallel process which will unfold in future centuries and culminate in the Most Great Peace.

Theirs is an exciting adventure — they will see the worst of times and the beginning of the best of times. The ending of the age-old period when wars seemed the only way to resolve conflicts among nations — and the new age, arrived at through tribulations, in which a Pact of non-aggression, involving every nation of the planet, will be upheld by those same nations.

Is this not a wonderful dream come true? Is this not a time when tribulation precedes joy?

Know the reason for the pain and tribulations of today, and the fruit of peace which will be born from these ordeals. Share it wisely with your children, as you hold them on your lap, in the security of your loving arms, with all the hope and confidence Bahá'u'lláh has instilled into our hearts. And we will attain the victory over our own selves and gain courage needed for these days leading ever closer to the establishment of the Lesser Peace.

Youth

Youth are in a much better position to understand the processes and forces operating in this critical period of human history. The Guardian appreciated their capacity to understand and prepare for this time of global suffering when he wrote in 1932 —

> "The present condition of the world, its economic instability, social dissensions, political dissatisfaction and international distrust should awaken the youth from their slumber and make them inquire what the future is going to bring. It is surely they who will suffer most if some calamity sweeps over the world. They should therefore open their eyes to the existing conditions, study the evil forces that are at work and then with a concerted effort arise and bring about the

necessary reforms — reforms that shall contain within their scope the spiritual as well as the social and political phase of human life."

(LG 508)

With regard to a basic hopeful and optimistic view of the future, the Guardian wrote this to the Youth Committee of the United States in 1945 —

"Above all, they should set a high example to them: chastity, politeness, friendliness, hospitality, joyous optimism about the ultimate future happiness and well-being of mankind, should distinguish themselves and win over to them the love and admiration of their fellow-youth."

(LG 508)

In 1932, a letter written on behalf of the beloved Guardian contrasted the Bahá'í with non-Bahá'í youth, particularly in their ability to perceive the processes at work in this climactic historic period —

"Whereas they [non-Bahá'í youth] see before them only a world that is crumbling down we are also seeing a new world being built up. Whereas they experience the destruction of old institutions that commanded their respect, we are beholding the dawn of a new era with its strict commands and new social bonds..."

(LG 515)

In more recent times the Universal House of Justice has pointed out the extraordinary role youth can play:

"You will live your lives in a period when the forces of history are moving to a climax, when mankind will see the establishment of the Lesser Peace, and during which the Cause of God will play an increasingly prominent role in the reconstruction of human society. It is you who will be called upon in the years to come to stand at the helm of the Cause in the face of conditions and developments which can, as yet, scarcely be imagined."

(UHJ, July 4, 1983)

With regard to the contributions present-day youth and future youth can play in the reconstruction of human society, the Supreme Institution wrote regarding the United Nations International Youth Year, 1985 —

"...The hope of the United Nations in thus focusing on youth is to encourage their conscious participation in the affairs of the world through their involvement in international development and such other undertakings and relationships as may aid the realization of their aspirations for a world without war.
"These expectations reinforce the immediate, vast opportunities begging our attention. To visualize, however imperfectly, the challenges that engage us now, we have only to reflect, in the light of our sacred Writings, upon the confluence of favorable circumstances brought about by the accelerated unfolding of the Divine Plan over nearly five decades, by the untold potencies of the spiritual drama being played out in Iran, and by the creative energy stimulated by awareness of the approaching end of the twentieth century. Undoubtedly, it is within your power to contribute significantly to shaping the societies of the coming century; youth can move the world."

(UHJ, January 3, 1984)

In a letter to the Bahá'í youth of the world the House of Justice alluded to the qualifications Bahá'í youth must acquire —

"We applaud those youth who, in respect of this period, have already engaged in some activity within their national and local communities or in collaboration with their peers in other countries, and call upon them to persevere in their unyielding efforts to acquire spiritual qualities and useful qualifications. For if they do so, the influence of their high-minded motivations will exert itself upon world developments conducive to a productive, progressive and peaceful future."

(UHJ, May 8, 1985)

In the following excerpt from the same letter, the youth are encouraged to distinguish themselves in order that they can make outstanding contributions to humanity at this critical point in its history —

"Indeed, let them welcome with confidence the challenges awaiting them. Imbued with this excellence and a corresponding humility, with tenacity and a loving servitude, today's youth must move towards the front ranks of the professions, trades, arts and crafts which are necessary to the further progress of humankind — this to insure that the spirit of the Cause will cast its illumination on all these important areas of human endeavour. Moreover, while aiming at mastering the unifying concepts and swiftly advancing technologies of this era of communications, they can, indeed, they must also guarantee the transmittal to the future of those skills which will preserve the marvelous, indispensable achievements of the past. The transformation which is to occur in the functioning of society will certainly depend to a great extent on the effectiveness of the preparations the youth make for the world they will inherit..."

The role of Bahá'í youth in shaping the future of society during the early years of the Lesser Peace will be that of bringing spiritual light to the political unifying processes that will be in operation. That the world will be politically, economically, and socially more sophisticated than the world which precedes the inception of the Lesser Peace is clear. On the spiritual level, mankind will have traversed the darkest period of the Age of Transition, and will have attained, as a result of worldwide afflictions and suffering, a new depth of spiritual development and insight. And having experienced that dark heart of the Age of Transition with conscious knowledge of God's purpose, as revealed in the Bahá'í Writings, the Bahá'í youth will have been groomed to continue to carry forth the light of Bahá'u'lláh's teachings into the age of the Lesser Peace. All efforts made to facilitate the spiritual transformation of society during the Lesser Peace will hasten its evolution and widen the foundations for the eventual unfoldment of the long-awaited Most Great Peace.

EPILOGUE

The Silver Lining

In the Riḍván message of 1988 the Universal House of Justice encourages the Baháʼís of the world with the following passage;

> "A silver lining to the dark picture which has overshadowed most of this century now brightens the horizon. It is discernible in the new tendencies impelling the social processes at work throughout the world, in the evidences of an accelerated trend toward peace. In the Faith of God, it is the growing strength of the Order of Baháʼuʼlláh as its banner rises to more stately heights. It is a strength that attracts."

In this passage those processes operating in both the major and the minor plans of God are highlighted. The major plan of God, operating through mankind as a whole is relentlessly propelling the world toward the Lesser Peace. The minor plan of God, working through the Baháʼís of the world and through Baháʼí institutions, is moving the Faith well beyond its former stage of obscurity into the light of public attention. This offers an opportunity to visibly demonstrate the efficacy of Baháʼuʼlláh's teachings in alleviating the social and spiritual problems afflicting our world.

The interplay between these two plans is continual and dynamic. As the world matures it moves toward peace — its inevitable destiny — and gradually moves towards the spiritual light which will eventually transform the Lesser Peace into the Most Great Peace. As the Lesser Peace is born and grows, it will welcome and seek out the warmth of the light of Bahá'u'lláh's healing Words.

As to the few years remaining before the close of the twentieth century, the Bahá'ís have a responsibility to share "The Promise of World Peace" with as many people on the planet as possible so as to create a general awareness in the minds of everyone that the Great Peace is at hand, but the path leading to that peace will be chosen by all of us.

> *"Whether peace is to be reached only after unimaginable horrors precipitated by humanity's stubborn clinging to old patterns of behavior, or is to be embraced now by an act of consultative will, is the choice before all who inhabit the earth..."*

(PWP, 1)

The opportunity to awaken humanity to the existence of such a choice, and to the weight and potential consequences of such a choice is one that presents itself to every Bahá'í, man, woman, youth, and child. This particular situation facing mankind at such a critical point in its history may never come again. The impact of this effort, i.e., awakening humanity to the necessity of making a choice as to which approach to the Lesser Peace it will take, is both obvious and beyond our imaginations. This historic effort on the part of the Bahá'ís of the world could make the difference as to the road mankind will travel.

BIBLIOGRAPHY

'Abdu'l-Bahá in Canada, Toronto, National Spiritual Assembly of the Bahá'ís of Canada, revised edition, 1987.

'Abdu'l-Bahá in London, London, Bahá'í Publishing Trust, 1982.

The Advent of Divine Justice, Shoghi Effendi, Wilmette, Bahá'í Publishing Trust, 1984.

Bahá'í Administration, Shoghi Effendi, Wilmette, Bahá'í Publishing Trust, 1968.

Bahá'í Prayers, Wilmette, Bahá'í Publishing Trust, 1982.

The Bahá'í World, Vol. XV, Haifa, Bahá'í World Centre, 1976.

The Bible, King James Version, Nashville/New York, Regency Publishing House, (Giant Reference Edition) 1979.

Citadel of Faith, Shoghi Effendi, Wilmette, Bahá'í Publishing Trust, second printing, 1970.

A Cry from the Heart, William Sears, Oxford, George Ronald, 1982.

The Divine Art of Living, Compiled by Mabel Hyde Paine, Wilmette, Bahá'í Publishing Trust, (4th revised edition), 1979.

The Dynamic Force of Example, Wilmette, Bahá'í Publishing Trust, 1974.

Gleanings from the Writings of Bahá'u'lláh', Bahá'u'lláh', Wilmette, Bahá'í Publishing Trust, 1976 edition, reprinted 1982.

God Passes By, Shoghi Effendi, Wilmette, Bahá'í Publishing Trust, (2nd printing), 1979.

The Hidden Words of Bahá'u'lláh', Bahá'u'lláh', Wilmette, Bahá'í Publishing Trust, 1979.

Kitáb-i-Iqán, Bahá'u'lláh', London, Bahá'í Publishing Trust, (3rd edition), 1982.

Lights of Guidance, compiled by Helen Hornby, New Delhi, Bahá'í Publishing Trust, 1983.

Messages to America, Shoghi Effendi, Wilmette, Bahá'í Publishing Trust, 1947.

Messages to the Bahá'í World, Shoghi Effendi, Wilmette, Bahá'í Publishing Trust, 1958, 1971.

Messages from the Universal House of Justice, Wilmette, Bahá'í Publishing Trust, 1976.

The Onward March of the Faith, National Spiritual Assembly of the Bahá'ís of the United Kingdom, London, Bahá'í Publishing Trust, 1975.

The Promise of World Peace, The Universal House of Justice, Haifa, Bahá'í World Centre, 1985.

The Promised Day is Come, Shoghi Effendi, Wilmette, Bahá'í Publishing Trust, 1980.

The Priceless Pearl, Rúhíyyih Rabbání, London, Bahá'í Publishing Trust, 1969.

Paris Talks, 'Abdu'l-Bahá, London, Bahá'í Publishing Trust, (11th edition), reprinted 1979.

BIBLIOGRAPHY

The Promulgation of Universal Peace, 'Abdu'l-Bahá, Wilmette, Bahá'í Publishing Trust, 1982.

Some Answered Questions, 'Abdu'l-Bahá, Wilmette, Bahá'í Publishing Trust, 1982.

The Secret of Divine Civilization, 'Abdu'l-Bahá, Wilmette, Bahá'í Publishing Trust, 1970, third printing 1983.

The Seven Valleys and the Four Valleys, Bahá'u'lláh, Wilmette, Bahá'í Publishing Trust, (3rd revised edition), 1978.

Selections from the Writings of 'Abdu'l-Bahá, Haifá, Bahá'í World Centre, 1978.

Tablets of 'Abdu'l-Bahá, 'Abdu'l-Bahá, Chicago, Bahá'í Publishing Society, 1909.

Tablets of Bahá'u'lláh, Bahá'u'lláh, Haifa, Bahá'í World Centre, 1978.

Victory Promises, William Sears, National Spiritual Assembly of the Bahá'ís of the Hawaiian Islands, 1978.

Wellspring of Guidance, Messages from the Universal House of Justice, 1963-1968, Wilmette, Bahá'í Publishing Trust, 1976.

World Order, Winter 1983-4, Wilmette, Bahá'í Publishing Trust, 1982.